Beginnings...

Teaching and Learning
in the Kindergarten

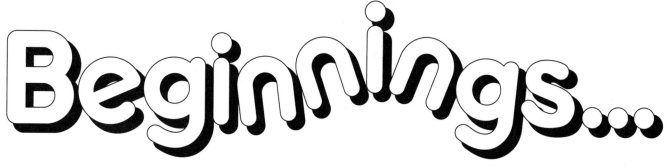

Beginnings...
Teaching and Learning
in the Kindergarten

RON BENSON

Foreword by Bill Martin, Jr.

Richard C. Owen Publishers, Inc.
Katonah, New York

Every effort has been made to find and acknowledge correctly the words of the songs reproduced in this book. The publisher welcomes any information that will enable him to rectify, in subsequent editions, any errors or omissions.

Library of Congress Cataloging-in-Publication Data
Benson, Ron, 1942-
    Beginnings- - teaching and learning in the kindergarten / Ron
Benson.
        p.   cm.
    Includes bibliographical references (p.).
    ISBN 1-878450-54-9
    1. Kindergarten- -Canada. 2. Benson, Ron, 1942-   - -Career in
teaching. I. Title. II. Title: Beginnings.
LB1241.B46 1993
372.21'8'0971- -dc20
                                                                93-20194
                                                                     CIP

Cover design by Julian Cleva
Illustrations by Julian Cleva
Edited by Norma Pettit
Cover photo by Dennis Broughton, Commercial Photography and Visual Images
Photographs by Dennis Broughton, Commercial Photography and Visual Images

Published by
Richard C. Owen Publishers, Inc.
135 Katonah Avenue
Katonah, New York 10536   Printed in the United States of America
                                            9 8 7 6 5 4 3 2

My thanks, my appreciation, and my love
to my children
Carolyn and Timothy,
who have brought, and continue to bring
such incredible joy to my life

And especially to Judie—for everything...and
so much more!

CONTENTS

Acknowledgements

Beginnings: Teaching and Learning in the Kindergarten has emerged as a result of knowing, and learning from, a number of people who, through the years, have influenced and enriched my professional and personal lives, and have helped me to grow both as a teacher and as a person. I would like to acknowledge and express my appreciation and gratitude to some of those people who, for me, have made a difference.

- Eric Hughes who gave me such a wonderful opportunity, and Sandra McCrossan and Joan Hazelwood, my kindergarten partners

- all those practising teachers who have been students in the Primary, Junior, and Reading Education courses I've taught through the past twenty-five years, and from whom I have learned, and continue to learn so much

- Janet Heagle who, early in my teaching career, supported and encouraged me in my work with young children, and showed me through her example, a program to which I shall always aspire

- Elaine, Maureen, Jill, Sherry, Joan, Claudette, Stephanie, Carolyn, Sue, Sandi, and Lois who give me such wonderful support and encouragement in my work, and whose talents as teachers and education consultants are truly remarkable

- John Ryckman who has taught me so much about the reading process through his questions, his answers, and his perceptive knowledge

- Sylvia Lee, whose wise counsel is appreciated, and whose friendship is very important to me

- The sixty-three student teachers who shared their pre-service year with me. Their enthusiasm and questions reminded me of the excitement and the concerns that "becoming teachers" have, when they realize that in less than a year, they will be responsible for the educational program and success of a group of youngsters. In particular, I thank the "group of twenty-three" who supported me throughout the year, gave me the opportunity to observe them in action with the children during their practice teaching placements, and convinced me that the future of education and teaching are in good hands.

- Bill Martin, Jr., for writing the Foreword to this book, for inspiring and challenging us all to know more about children and their learning, and for understanding what really matters in the classroom and telling about it in *The Human Connection*.

- my friend Paul who has always been there for almost forty years

- and, of course, those twenty-two four- and five-year-olds who shared their young lives with me so I could learn!

I would also like to acknowledge some of the people at Irwin Publishing who have helped me to see this project through from inception to completion. A very sincere thank you to Michael Davis and Terry Nikkel for giving me the "go-ahead" to this wonderful opportunity along with their support and encouragement. In particular, I wish to acknowledge Norma Pettit and Tom Sepp. To Norma, I extend my thanks and appreciation for the time, for the caring, and for the very focused and thoughtful consideration given to each of the many draft manuscripts along the way. Your pages of suggestions were always welcomed as you worked with me and helped me to make the message clearer. And to Tom, my thanks for the initial telephone call that put the process in motion, and for the support, encouragement, and direction through those early months during which the manuscript began to take shape. Above all, I have appreciated your belief in the message of this book; you have always made me feel that it was important.

And most certainly I want to acknowledge my appreciation to my employer, the Scarborough Board of Education. I am always very proud to say that I am an employee of the Scarborough educational system because I believe that it is a system of people who care very much about education, and who take the job of education very seriously. The opportunities and experiences, and the encouragement, direction, and support that I have received throughout my career with Scarborough from the trustees, the senior administration, the principals, and the many wonderful teachers with whom I've worked, have been both incredible and valued.

Ron Benson
Toronto 1992

Foreword

If you wonder how you fit into a child's kindergarten world, or conversely, how a child fits into the brace of conventions and opportunities that you conceive as kindergarten, then you're reading the right book. It enlivens me to covet its impact on you.

The author is Ron Benson. He's a kindergarten specialist. But he also is a child psychologist, a counselor, a wise observer. Especially he is a friend of children.

In *Beginnings*, Mr. Benson considers kindergarten with kaleidoscopic vision, beginning with the physical setting that houses both the child and the learning opportunities. He believes the kindergarten community is an empowering humanity that questions, challenges, extracts, extends, and juxtaposes the mix of teachers, parents, and children.

He concludes that the child is both the process and the product of kindergarten education, and that all else is hand servant to the miracle.

Here is a book that deserves our meditation and participation.

Bill Martin, Jr.
New York
November 1992

PART I:
The Setting

Beginnings: Teaching and Learning in the Kindergarten is a story about kindergarten and my experiences teaching and learning with four- and five-year-olds. Because kindergarten teaching is unlike any other teaching experience one can have, it's important that kindergarten teachers have a means of talking with one another so they can share their unique professional experiences and responsibilities. This book has provided me with an opportunity to talk to others who understand about kindergarten. Also, it has given me the time to reflect on myself as a teacher of a group of four- and five-year-olds.

I believe that teachers of any grade, as well as school and central office administrators, can learn so much about *real* learning from kindergarten children, and about *real* teaching from kindergarten teachers. And so, I hope that this book will reach not only prospective kindergarten teachers who are now in the faculties of education and those kindergarten teachers who are already practising their art, but also those administrators who share my belief that good programming across the elementary grades should be based on the kindergarten model.

Quite naturally, *Beginnings* is a different story from those stories that kindergarten teachers have told in the past and from those to be told in years to come, because every kindergarten is different, every year is different, school communities are different, and of course, all children and teachers are different. And yet I'm certain there will be situations described that are very similar to those you've had, are having, or will have as you move through life with the young learners in your charge. I do hope that you will be able to find yourself on many of the pages and in many of the situations described, as it would be satisfying to have others share my beliefs about working with children and my ideas about programming for the young.

It has been so exciting for me to have this opportunity to think back on that wonderful year—that extraordinary year in the kindergarten. As I set these words to the page, my mind is filled with so many pictures...

the children coming to school and seeing me
for the first time...they were so little...
and I was so nervous!

the tidy kindergarten as we started our days...
and the mess we were able to create together
in such a short time...

all the stories we shared...

having to replenish the white glue over and over and
over again!

There are so many memories.

But most of all, I remember two things—the music and the laughter. I can hear the children singing and laughing as if they were here with me right now.

In the June before I set out on my journey as a kindergarten teacher, I was vice principal at my school with teaching responsibilities in Grades 3 and 4. Towards the end of that June, we realized that because of the number of new senior kindergarten registrations for the following September, we were going to have many more senior kindergarten children than we had earlier projected. In fact, the numbers made it necessary for us to establish a third afternoon kindergarten unit (class). I went to Eric, my principal, and expressed an interest in teaching in the kindergarten. I had expected that he would want to talk my proposal over with me and then suggest that we both take a couple of days to think about it. Instead, without hesitation, he said, *"Sure. It sounds like a great idea!"*

My previous teaching experience had given me the opportunity to teach across the grades from Grade 1 to Grade 8. With that experience, I should have had all the confidence necessary to take on a group of four- and five-year-olds...but I didn't! I think I was secretly hoping that Eric would either say *"No,"* or that he would talk me out of it. But instead, within the space of a few seconds, my teaching fate for the following year had been sealed...there was no turning back.

I was going to teach kindergarten!

With that decision so firmly made, certain thoughts about teaching in the kindergarten began to have immediate appeal for me...far away from the rest of the school (to give me time to "find my roots" on my own), lots of opportunities to read and sing with the children (two of my favourite school things to do), and looking forward to what I thought would be a lack of the parental pressures that teachers in the grades often face. However, I was soon to find out that there **are** pressures—they are just different ones.

It seemed to me that as the school's vice principal, I would have the best of both worlds—doing the administrative kinds of things in the morning, and practising the art of teaching every afternoon. In fact, the more I thought about it, the more excited I got, and I found myself eager for the current school year to end so I would be closer to the challenge that awaited me.

About the School

The school in which I was teaching housed about 550 children from junior kindergarten to Grade 6, and was one of about 125 elementary schools in the jurisdiction. The school was an open-plan design located in a professional suburban community. Most of the children came from two-parent families and had a Christian background.

Eric, the principal of the school, provided wonderful encouragement to teachers and children. He was eager to hear our plans and ideas for programming, and he expected that we would work hard, take our jobs seriously, and bring a sense of humour to our work. He was a true protector of childhood, and he took delight in complimenting the children on their behaviour and their accomplishments. He never put excessive demands on his teaching staff, but he expected our loyalty to the children, to him, and to the school.

The staff was a cohesive group of hard-working and talented individuals. The open-plan construction of the building was instrumental in bringing the teachers together because everyone worked in a teaching area with at least one other teacher, and by the nature of the design all teaching areas from Grades 1 to 6 opened onto the corridor that formed the perimeter of the school. As a result, these classrooms were easily accessible and visible to everyone. The kindergarten area, which consisted of a large double room that could be divided into two smaller rooms, was separated from the other teaching areas. Unlike the other classrooms, the kindergartens opened onto the school library, the corridor that surrounded the teaching areas, and the foyer and school office.

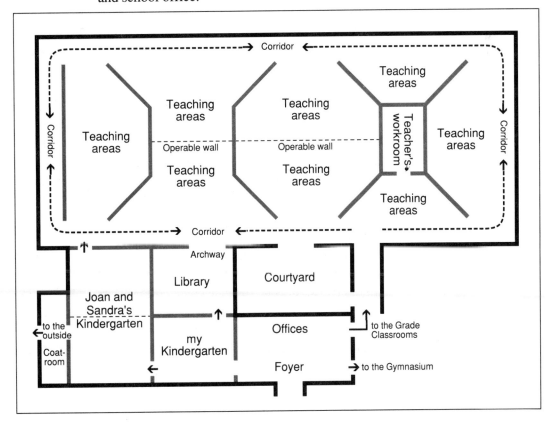

Although I had anticipated enjoying the sense of respite offered by the separation of the kindergarten area from the rest of the school, I later came to feel differently. I often tell people when recalling my year as a kindergarten teacher that in this situation I learned the true meaning of loneliness. Unless they absolutely had to, no one ever came near the kindergarten room. Those who did would always stay near the door—usually on the outside! I guess people just didn't understand how anyone would be able to talk to children who aren't proficient readers and writers.

The children in the school where I was teaching were the same mix of personalities that one finds in any school. There were those who were achievement-oriented and those who would have preferred to be anywhere but at school. There were those who excelled at sports and those who were talented in various areas of the arts. There were those who were happy and seemingly well adjusted, and those who were more troubled.

The school had a tradition of academic achievement and those expectations began in the kindergarten. Many of the kindergarten children came from homes where reading, writing, and mathematics were valued as the basics for eventual success in life. There was an expectation that academic learning would be promoted in the earliest years, and that the kindergarten program would be designed in response to this expectation.

Our classroom programs in the school were based on a child-centred philosophy, and the heart of the child-centred program in our kindergartens were the learning centres. (For more about learning centres in the kindergarten, see pages 105-11.) These were areas in the room that were set up to reflect different components of the curriculum. The number and locations of the learning centres were changed several times throughout the year in response to the interests of the children and their developing capabilities. Our kindergartens had many centres including painting, cut and paste, crayoning, writing, reading, blocks, building, math, sand, water, tapes and listening post, television, dress-up and drama, the house centre, music, science....As well, there was a "Special Centre" that changed every week. This was the centre at which parent volunteers, senior citizen helpers and other volunteers often spent some of their time because usually the activities at this centre required special instructions and often included a demonstration component. Recycling paper, papier mâché, finger painting, off-loom weaving, and making musical instruments were a few of the special activities that were available at different times through the year. As with all the learning centres, these special experiences were optional for the children. What happens throughout the year at the learning centres in terms of child-material interaction, teacher-child interaction, child to child and child to teacher language development is fascinating, revealing, and the basis for each child's growth.

The parents wanted the best for their children and they monitored our work carefully to make certain that the quality of the education we provided was of paramount importance to us. In turn, they took a personal interest in us as people, and they gave us overwhelming support as teachers when we needed volunteers to work in the kindergarten or to drive small groups of children on an excursion. They also responded in large numbers to invitations for them to attend parent/teacher interviews or Open Houses. And their questions about education really kept us on our toes and up-to-date in our professional reading.

Mine was a great school in which to teach. It was a school that was filled with challenge. With the challenge came tremendous personal reward for us, as teachers, from our principal, the community, and the children. Certainly, the school provided a wonderful setting for my first venture into kindergarten teaching.

About Joan and Sandra—My Kindergarten Partners

Not only was I very lucky as a first-time kindergarten teacher to be in the particular school in which I worked, I was extremely lucky in my kindergarten partners. As a great supporter of collaboration, I was very fortunate to have Joan and Sandra to work with during my first year in the kindergarten because they too enjoyed working with others rather than working in isolation.

Joan had been teaching full time in the kindergarten in our school, and early in June, Sandra, an experienced kindergarten teacher returning to teaching after a leave-of-absence, had been hired to teach in the afternoons beginning the next September. Because the decision for me to teach kindergarten was made near the end of June, and because a new and separate kindergarten room adjoining the large double room had to be constructed during the summer, the three of us did not have the opportunity to get together for any in-depth planning prior to the end of the school year. Our first time to plan cooperatively had to wait until later in August. However, before the school year ended, we did agree that Sandra and Joan would work together in the open double room with their two groups of children and that I would stay on my own with my group in the new room.

As well, at this initial end-of-June meeting, Joan was extremely helpful in giving me suggestions for timetabling. She urged me *to organize my timetable in blocks of time, with the major portion of time being set aside for the children to work at the learning centres of their choice.* As well, she gave me some ideas about routines that would help me to ease into kindergarten. She suggested, for example, that *I begin and end the class with the children coming together as a group, and that I keep rules to a minimum.* Because my room wasn't built, I really didn't have a sense of how it would look, where the electrical outlets would be, how many learning centres I would be able to set up, and so forth, so Joan just suggested that *I make sure that there would be a lot of floor space available—not only for the children to come together, but also for them to use as a working surface.* She said that many kindergarten children prefer to work on the floor rather than at tables and that I could probably do with fewer tables and more floor space.

When we were finally able to get together in the latter part of August, Sandra and Joan planned their first day while I listened in and made notes, so that I could follow the same routine and pattern that they were establishing.

Throughout the first term much of our interaction was of a more informal nature. Each day after school, as we went about the business of making our plans and preparing the environment for the next day, we would talk back and forth through the open door about how the day had gone, what the children were doing at the learning centres, and about the particular interests the children in our respective groups were showing in the different centres. My most frequently asked question to Sandra and Joan was, *"What do you do when...?"* and they were both very patient in describing how I could best handle the child who moved from centre to centre without bringing anything to closure, how to keep my group times brief, and how to distribute the huge collection of work that accumulated at the end of each day and somehow had to get into the rightful owner's hands to be taken home!

Although at the time it seemed like an inconvenience, the fact that I had no cupboards for the storage of extra materials and equipment meant that everything was kept next door in Joan and Sandra's kindergarten, necessitating frequent visits by me not only before and after school, but also during kindergarten hours when my group needed more paint or construction paper or....These trips for supplies gave me wonderful—albeit very brief—opportunities to see their program in action, to catch glimpses of them working with the children, and to learn on the spot.

One routine we did develop together early in the year was to visit the school library after school every other day to choose books to read to the children and to put in our book corners. With our school librarian's help, each of us was able to collect books that related to what the children were talking about and thus we were able to keep our book corners reflective of the current interests of the children. It was extremely helpful that the library was next door to the kindergartens and that our librarian, Kathy, was so keen about books and reading and people that she welcomed our regular visits and willingly joined in the search with us.

Joan, Sandra, and I developed compatible timetables so that our times for working directly with the children and our times when the children were working more independent of us were the same. This arrangement allowed us to roam into each others' rooms to observe the respective programs in action and to interact with and get to know all the children.

The planning and preparation for the Christmas Concert was our first truly collaborative undertaking. Because of this collaboration, we synchronized the organization of our days even more, so that we could bring all the children together for practice times beginning in the kindergarten and then, eventually, in the auditorium. It was this experience of working very closely together that made us realize that we wanted to combine the children and the programs so that we could work together throughout the day.

And so, from early December onward, the three of us met every day after school to plan how—we hoped!—the next day would evolve. Collaboratively we decided on the physical arrangement of the two rooms, and we organized a timetable that would allow us to have some times with our own groups of children—to talk about the plans for the day, to read to them, to talk with them, and to have a sharing time with them before they went home each day. We combined our music times, snack times, show-and-tell times, and learning centre blocks of time. In addition, we were able to work out with the rest of the staff an arrangement that would allow our gym times to follow one another. That organization permitted us to take smaller or larger groups to the gym at any one time, for each of us to take another's group, and sometimes, for one of us to take three successive groups of children to the gym while the other two teachers stayed in the kindergarten with the remaining two groups of children.

Because our planning became more cooperative and collaborative, we were able to make more efficient use of time for organizing purposes. Each of us would assume responsibility, on a weekly basis, for particular centres and particular learning experiences.

Sandra and I enjoyed the music time, so we would share that planning. Joan enjoyed the preparations involved in setting up the Special Table at which a special craft would be offered, so she often took responsibility for that activity. For the Science Fair, Sandra wrote the letter to the parents describing what we were going to do, and how and why we were doing it; Joan took the responsibility for creating a large area near the windows where sixty-eight containers for our Growing unit could be set up, and my responsibility was to design and organize the method of recording the daily observations. We rotated show-and-tell responsibilities, and when springtime came we took turns supervising our children during recess, and sometimes we went out together with the children for the recess period. We also shared the writing of letters to the parents to notify them of upcoming excursions, special materials we needed, or upcoming special events in the school. And together we ordered films and videotapes and our consumable materials.

The three of us were very open in our expressions of satisfactions and dissatisfactions with certain components of the program and, as a result, we were able to make ongoing changes that we thought were necessary and possible.

For me, however, the highlight of our times together was when we talked about the children and the program. I benefitted so much from the experience of Joan and Sandra, particularly when we talked together about reasonable expectations in various areas of the curriculum. We would look at sample pieces of art together and they would help me to understand the stage of the child's development. We talked about individual children's responses to various learning opportunities.... *"Did you notice that Ian volunteered to work on the mural with Chris today?"* And we talked about programming possibilities for children who seemed to need great challenge. Both Joan and Sandra had a storehouse of materials and ideas accumulated from their previous teaching experiences in kindergarten, and they shared both with me very generously.

From our regular and ongoing meeting times together throughout the year, not only was I able to gain a lot of insights into teaching kindergarten, but also I learned to feel more comfortable with what I was doing through the support, encouragement, and the specific direction and advice that Joan and Sandra gave me.

Getting Ready

In the year in which I was to teach kindergarten, our school had five kindergarten classes—two junior kindergarten classes of three- and four-year-olds in the morning, and three senior kindergarten classes of four- and five-year-olds in the afternoon. I was to teach one of the afternoon senior kindergarten classes. As it happened, I was to be the first male to teach kindergarten in our system.

The first challenge the school faced, once we realized that we were going to need a third senior kindergarten class, was to find a space suitable for a group of twenty or more four- and five-year-olds. The original design of the building had only provided enough space for two groups of kindergarten children in a large double room, or, by closing a moveable wall, in two separate groups. The space was sufficient for our two junior kindergarten classes in the morning, but the need for a third kindergarten class in the afternoon required that we find a third space. So we began by making the necessary plans to combine half the library with adjoining hall space to create a third "kindergarten" area. (The quotation marks simply indicate that by putting up walls, you really don't get a room suitable for four- and five-year-olds!) A door that opened from this new room to the large open double room would join the programs, the sixty-eight children, and the three teachers.

The second challenge was to order equipment and materials for the children to use in the new kindergarten. Wouldn't it be wonderful if the money supply were endless so that everything we wanted—and thought we needed—for the kindergarten could be purchased...no questions asked?! But, as we know, that isn't the way real life is. However, in my Board we do have what is called a start-up budget available to schools that are opening new classrooms. The amount varies from grade to grade and is determined by costing out what is listed by the Board as necessary material and equipment for the particular level. This list, which is available to all schools, provides an excellent starting point for ordering when one is new to the particular teaching assignment, as I was. It is not necessary to order what is on the list; the only stipulation is that the order not exceed the amount provided by the Board's central office.

In my situation, I was teaching in a school that was well stocked with supplies and equipment, and before I decided what I needed to order for my new classroom, I raided the supply cupboards and book storage rooms looking for anything put on the shelves by other teachers because they no longer had any use for it, that could be used by four- and five-year-olds. To my amazement, I found some puzzles, counting materials, a few abacuses, plastic hosing, an aquarium, and some hand lenses—including a large "floor model" type!

Now it was time to decide: What additional supplies and equipment would I need? Who would help me decide? It was already summer and no one was around—everyone was on vacation. Get out the catalogues.

NO...first think about four- and five-year-olds. What are they like? What do they like? What do they need? Make copious lists. Read about kindergartens and kindergarten-aged children and find out what the experts have to say.

Then look at catalogues.

There was sure a lot of great material and equipment available for purchase, but even with the start-up funds available, my budget wouldn't allow me to buy it all. I had to exercise restraint and establish priorities.

- blocks (number 1 on my list!)
- sand and water
- puzzles
- paints
- easels
- puppets
- games

- construction toys—oh, oh—little cars, four- and five-year-olds love these
- some tables and chairs (get stacking tables so they can be piled in a corner when they're not needed)
- rummage through my closet for all my old suits, pants, shoes, jackets (I knew there was a reason for saving them—little children love to dress up), and ask my wife for dresses, hats and jewellery
- get the neighbours involved—save *all* cartons, boxes, tins, rolls; I'll take everything and we'll have a junk centre!

I also decided that I would send a letter home with the children at the beginning of the school year asking the children's parents to read the list I was including with the letter and to send in any materials for which they no longer had any use.

September

Dear Families,

As the children and I settle into our new kindergarten room I am realizing how much we could use your help in adding to our collection of materials. If you have any of the items listed below for which you no longer have any use, or if you come across some things that you think the children could use (please don't send us your best!), please send them along with your child. Your contributions will be gratefully received at any time throughout the year!

. tin cans, babyfood jars and plastic containers, with lids if possible (for paints and the storage of counting materials and inventions)

. pieces of lumber (suitable for use at the workbench)

. egg cartons (for sorting activities and creative artwork)

. needles and thread (for the sewing centre—there's certainly a lot of interest in learning how to thread a needle)

. pieces of scrap material (for sewing practice and for making clothes for the puppets)

. TV dinner trays (for portable paint stations and sorting and classifying activities)

. broken watches, clocks, etc. (for taking-apart purposes)

. worn-out small appliances with the plugs removed (for taking apart, or for the house centre)

.../2

...⁄2

    . buttons, record centres (for 45s) or anything else that could be
used for counting
    . easy puzzles and some that are a little bit harder (for practice
in matching the shape of the space with the shape of the puzzle piece)
    . well-used books (for browsing)
    . old keys and locks (for matching keys to locks)
    . etc.
        We're also looking for a worn-out television set with the picture
tube removed that we could use as a puppet stage, and large empty boxes
with which the children can build (Has your child told you about the
apartment building that three of the children built using refrigerator
crating and an assortment of smaller boxes that they are now standing
on chairs to paint green?).
        Please let me know if you have any of these larger items, and
I'll be happy to arrange to pick them up.
        Thank you for your support and your interest in our program.

        Sincerely,

OK, ordering is finished. We'll see how we do.

What's this? It's just a week until the children arrive and the builders are just finishing the walls—and the electricians still haven't got us hooked up. We'll just have to work around them.

The room's a mess but I'm anxious to get going. Where will I put the furniture and the equipment that have arrived? (Most, as usual, is still in some company's stockroom. I hope it gets here before the year is over!) How do you organize a kindergarten room? Joan and Sandra are away. I think I'll visit my friend Terry who teaches in a nearby Board and has lots of kindergarten experience. She'll help me out.

Sure enough, she's ready for me and out we go one evening in late August to see her kindergarten. Wow! So neatly organized—a place for everything and this room has everything!

But I'm not Terry so I can't organize myself or the kindergarten in the way she does. But she answers that everything will be great and that I'll do OK. I feel better. It's really important to have teaching colleagues who give you support and encouragement when you need it. And do I ever need it! I am getting nervous about last-minute preparations.

Roll in a spare and available piano. Every child deserves music and lots of it. Find a tape recorder and some earphones. Where will I put them? Best idea—near a plug! Order films and videotapes to get us started. Make some board games that I found described in our Board's kindergarten program guides. Gather up mirrors and microscopes, sponges and straws, buttons and pattern blocks...anything I think will appeal to my fours and fives. I wonder what the children on my class list will look like? I'll bet they're all sizes and colours; some very verbal, others quiet. Make them happy—that's my first job. Let them know that I'm an OK person—I think so—let them know that they're OK too. Give them lots of encouragement and support to get us started.

A few more hours spent in the kindergarten room and I'm all set—well, as ready as I can be for the time being anyway!

(For more about getting ready for the school year, see pages 112-13.)

And now—*travel back with me to that wonderful year in the kindergarten!*

A Year in the Kindergarten
...and What a Year It Was!!

First Term: The Year Begins!

What is kindergarten? Literally translated it's a "child's garden" and that's just what I hope I can make it for the children I'm going to teach. For the four- or five-year-old child, first experiences at school should extend for the child what every kindergarten teacher hopes is a beautiful life outside the school filled with play, physical activity, social interaction, and sunshine. We're simply going to move indoors! And for those children whose lives have not been as joyful, I hope that I'll be able to bring some happiness to their days.

My children will be coming every afternoon from 1:00 to 3:30. But on the first day of school, the afternoon is set aside for professional development so I won't meet my children until day two. I'll spend my first morning doing vice principal kinds of things—finding materials for teachers, taking new children to classes—ninety new children are registering so my mind will be occupied.

In the afternoon, I'll do some last-minute preparations and organization, and talk to Joan and Sandra who will be working together in the big room and whose help to me during the past week, in anticipation of school opening, has been appreciated. I've decided to stay on my own for a while until I get the feeling of the flow in a kindergarten. I need some time to get to know my group of children and to feel more at ease with "how kindergarten goes." I have so many questions to answer—What can the children do? What are their interests? How long can they sustain their interest and involvements?—but the questions can only be answered by the children. Be patient, they'll be here tomorrow and some of the mysteries will be solved and my anxieties allayed...I hope!

It's almost 1:00 day two. The moment to be reckoned with. All the senior kindergarten children are waiting outdoors—many with adult hands to hold. Some of the adults look more frightened than their children. Joan, who teaches junior kindergarten in the morning and senior kindergarten in the afternoon, is the only "holdover" from last year. The parents know her—trust her. But Sandra and "the man" are new to the kindergarten. The letter sent out during August has informed the parents and the children of the teacher's name. *"What's this—a male kindergarten teacher?"*

I'm intrigued by the several children outside with no adults or older brothers or sisters to hold their hands. Are four- and five-year-olds that secure, that independent? If they can stand alone on their first day, imagine the self-confidence they must have. Bravo! (I wish I had as much!)

We open the doors and the children timidly come into the large room...I timidly wait. Little faces and bodies appear quietly. It's a beautiful day so no coats are needed. (Oops—I must remember to label the coat hooks with the children's names!) Tentatively all the children group around the rocking chair that Joan has strategically placed in a large open space. They wait and wonder. A little welcoming song and the year has begun.

It's my turn. I read aloud the names from my class list. Now I'll be able to match the names with the faces. My children and I collect at the orange door that leads into our kindergarten. Twenty-two little bodies of enthusiasm—one big body of apprehension. In we go together to do some more sitting. Match faces with the name cards I've prepared. Many recognize their names—they've already begun to read! Cheers for them. Pascale, a French-Canadian child who doesn't speak one word of English, looks frightened. She doesn't understand. A big thank you in my mind to my high school French teachers who gave me sufficient skill to communicate with this beautiful little five-year-old. *"Bonjour, comment ça va?"* That's all we seem to need for the moment to get us started.

Name Cards

Using strips of Bristol board approximately 7.5 cm x 20 cm and a black magic marker, I prepared a name card for each of the children and had the collection ready on the first day as a way of showing the children that I was expecting them. On the front side, I used the conventional format of upper- and lower-case letters to print the child's first name and surname initial. On the reverse side, I printed the first name and surname initial totally in upper-case lettering. If the child didn't recognize the conventional print I turned the card over to see if the upper-case lettering brought recognition. Because many, if not most, children begin to print their names using upper-case letters exclusively, some don't recognize their names in the conventional format. By printing the child's name using both formats, the child, over time, will learn to recognize his or her name in both forms.

For those children who had recently registered and whose names did not appear on the prepared class list, I had extra Bristol board cards available and I printed their names on the spot!

For more about name cards and how they can be used in the classroom as learning opportunities, see pages 80-1.

After meeting the children and talking briefly to them about the various learning centres in the kindergarten, I invite them to choose where they wish to play and work...and they're off! I spend my time roaming about the room trying to match faces with names as well as seeing what the children do with the materials and equipment available to them. My first observation is that

they are very energetic and that they move from centre to centre easily...and frequently! Two and a half hours later we find we've survived. Teach them the beautiful "Good-Bye" song from *Scissors and Songs*, with small hands folded, and we're ready for home.

Before we go away,
We'll fold our hands and pray
That [we will all be] safe
   and well
Until another day.

Good-Bye! Good-Bye,
Until another day!
[Good-Bye! Good-Bye,
Until another day!]

"Good-Bye" from Scissors *and Songs (Part One)* by Claire Senior Burke.
© Copyright 1936 by Gordon V. Thompson Music, A Division of
Warner/Chappell Music Canada Ltd., Toronto Canada.
Reprinted by kind permission.

I'm exhausted...the children are lively. I'm ready for another holiday; they're ready to get on with the year! They've taken it all in their stride. I think they could tell I was unsure but they're letting me work it through.

How kind the children are.

I think I'm going to love this year.

I have decided to use different colours each month as one way to integrate the children's learning. Yellow is our September colour and our Colour Table is filled with yellow things brought in by the children and me. We look and touch. A big yellow happy face hangs down from our ceiling. Even when our colour changes, the happy face will remain.

The Colour of the Month

At the beginning of each month I covered a table and a display panel with construction paper to advertise "the colour of the month." On the table I put an assortment of objects of the same colour, and I put a collection of pictures that featured the colour on the display panel that formed a backdrop to the table. The children were invited to add to the table collection throughout the month and to contribute artwork to the panel display. I made cards and magic markers available so the children could print their names on a card and put the card with the object to ensure its return—sometimes at the end of the day, often at the end of the week, and occasionally at the end of the month. I also set up a work table nearby with art and writing materials (paint, construction paper, Play Dough, crayons, magic markers, coloured pencils, blank pages inside a construction paper cover of the featured colour) so the children could choose to work with materials that corresponded to the colour of the month.

After introducing the colour table, the display board, and the work table to the children in September, little more needed to be said about the routine throughout the year. The children brought in objects from home or those they found on the way to school, and made a name card to put on or under the object to identify the owner.

I found having a colour of the month to be an effective way of generating talk about colour, and without the tedium of teaching the colours to the few children who did not yet recognize them, of generating discussions about and focusing attention on the colours in a more natural and purposeful way. Many of the children, however, could already recognize, name, and discriminate colours. For them the activity became an opportunity to experiment with colour using various art media, and to think about the presence of colour both in their homes and in the outside environment. The colour of the month table and related activities were available throughout the year for browsing and self-selected involvement by the children as a way of allowing the children to focus on the presence of the colour in their lives.

On the first day of each month we would gather around the colour centre and talk about the colour for the month and why it was an appropriate colour to think about that month. We'd look at the few objects I'd brought in to start the collection, and the pictures I'd put up on the display panel; and we'd look at the materials available on the work table for them to use. On occasion throughout the month, I would build time into the day for us to look together at a particular object that was unusual or, perhaps, unexpected.

On the last day of the month we celebrated the colour by wearing clothes, singing songs, and listening to stories that featured the colour. Objects on the table and artwork and colour booklets on the display panel were returned to the children.

As the year progressed, we would talk about the month that was to begin the next day and I would have the children guess which colour was going to be featured for the month. I would print the various possibilities suggested on chart paper, and the children would guess the one they thought I would be choosing, and I would record their votes in tally form.

As the children became more aware of special days that were coming up in the next month or the kind of weather we were likely to have, they were able to anticipate my selection with greater accuracy and they delighted in telling me that they had guessed right.

During this first month with the children I am learning so much. Most of all, I'm learning how different the children all are. Some love crafts...some show no interest at all. Some love the alphabet, others don't have any idea what it is—those funny lines that are supposed to mean something. Marianne loves to sing...and on key too! Robbie can read and Sandra can hardly wait to learn. Jason likes to listen and Ian loves to love. So different they all are. But every child is willing to give me a chance and it's during this first month that I know I must prove myself to the children. But I can't do that until I have total confidence in myself...and the children seem so willing to give me the time I need.

We spend most of our time each day learning and sharing together at the classroom learning centres—painting, colouring, cutting and pasting, block building, playing house, experimenting and discovering, listening to story tapes, looking at books....Four- and five-year-olds do a better job of choosing an activity and moving from one activity to another than do many of the older children I have taught. Their lives outside school have been filled with choices and decisions and they know how to direct themselves.

We have been blessed with beautiful weather during our September days. Every day we go outside to the park adjoining the schoolyard to swing and slide and climb and run. How the children love this time. I get to know them better...

"Push me..."
"Higher..."
"Stop..."
"Watch me, watch me, watch me!"

We have wonderful times outside. I think I enjoy these moments more than the children do. Whoever looked after that glorious September sunshine...thank you.

Tradition tells us in our Board that a Curriculum/Meet-the-Teacher Night will be a part of our September each year. We schedule ours for the last Wednesday of the month. What shall I do? How will I share my feelings, my enthusiasms, my joys with the moms and dads?

"A picture is worth a thousand words."

That's it! Take slides. The pictures will speak for themselves. I hope the children will smile while I'm snapping them.

The night comes. We have our time in the auditorium. All the staff and all the parents together. The staff is introduced. Eric (our principal) makes very supportive remarks about our school because he believes in children and he believes in teachers too. I choose a suit with red-checked pants and vest and black jacket to brighten up my evening!

Following Eric's presentation, the parents are invited to visit the classrooms to hear about the program from their children's teachers. Sandra and Joan are in their kindergarten together. I'm alone in mine. The time comes and the room quickly fills up. Standing room only.

I knew it. Curiosity has won out, for many of the people there—as I was to find out later—were not parents of children I was teaching.

I show my slides of the children at their work in the kindergarten accompanied by taped background music and then, using prepared overlays to guide the presentation, I talk my way through a "typical" day in the kindergarten putting special emphasis on the value of play as a way of learning and the role of the various learning centres in supporting the children's learning. But I present myself and the program guardedly. I try to convince the parents that I'm right for the job.

I survive the evening but I'm not pleased. I was too defensive. My voice revealed my anxiety. Did I settle people's minds or further agitate them?

The next morning I receive two phone calls from parents—both fathers! Each sensed my anxiety and responded. Both give me their full support. I'm very happy about constructively concerned parents. I feel better.

Now we can settle down to our school routine and get on with the job at hand—the day-to-day living and learning in the kindergarten. The beautiful sunshine days continue, and our daily trips outside are anticipated with delight by the children and me. We have good fun together and we share life—the ups and the downs and the realities of twenty-three people living together for two and a half hours a day, five days a week.

About Robbie, Sandra, Peter, and Cindy

These four children in particular provided me with the challenge of trying to satisfy their academic curiosities. Each was bright, alert, and very self-motivated to learn—not in a pressing, urgent kind of way, but rather, just as a matter of course in their daily lives. They seemed to come to kindergarten with the expectation that not only *should* they learn beyond where their learning had taken them in their lives outside school but that they *would*, and that opportunities to know more and to be able to do more would be available to them. They all had high personal expectations of themselves, and each wanted to succeed. In spite of their common desire to learn, they were very different children:

Robbie:
- an only child
- the only child in the class who could read on the opening day of school
- had a small group of loyal friends
- asked *"Why"*—a lot!
- had a well-developed vocabulary for a child his age and spoke precisely and distinctly
- was very socially conscious and was easily embarrassed if he had to be reminded of something when others were nearby to hear

Sandra:
- younger of two daughters
- very intellectually curious
- enjoyed mathematical challenges and card tricks!
- although serious about her learning, she took it all in her stride and didn't seem to let anything bother her too much
- very willing to take risks and to try anything new—especially if there was an element of mystery involved
- always in motion!

Peter:
- the youngest of three boys
- very curious about mathematics—especially numbers, and natural science—*"Why is the sky blue some days and grey some days?"*
- hesitant to try anything new until he knew exactly how it was to be done, or how it worked, or what was expected of him
- extremely popular with the other children
- very cooperative, courteous, responsible, and reliable
- sensitive to the feelings of others
- able to tell time and always "ready"—he seemed to have a sixth sense about when it was time to go to the centres, to the gym, to clean up, etc., and he would often remind me when we got behind schedule (he reminded me frequently!)

Cindy:
- youngest child in the family; two older brothers
- January birthday, so older than most of the others in the class
- very settled and calm
- good oral vocabulary; however, preferred to be a listener
- very cooperative and courteous
- had one very close friend
- preferred academic pursuits (for example, reading, writing, mathematics) to artistic involvements
- preferred self-selected learning experiences in which she could work alone or with her close friend
- hesitant to engage in anything new; avoided risk-taking

- a decided preference for mental engagements over physical activities

With the exception of Robbie, for their first choice each of these children generally selected an activity one might call academic: Cindy usually selected a pencil-to-paper task, Peter chose something in the math centre, and Sandra went regularly to the book corner. Robbie, however, chose blocks or painting or dress-up.

What I found worked best for me was to make certain I spent a little time with these four children individually during the learning centre time to talk about *what* they were doing, and *how* and *where* their work was going. My involvement with each was something for which I couldn't prepare ahead of time because I didn't know for certain **where** they would choose to work or **what** they would be doing at the centres. So I would begin with the old standby question, *"What are you doing?"* and then, depending on the content of the response, decide how, or if, I should become involved. Many times the child would ask a question and that would give me the direction I needed. For example, Cindy was very insistent that whatever she wrote be spelled correctly and that her letters be formed properly, so she would often ask, *"How do you spell...?"* or *"How do you make the letter...?"* Peter frequently wanted me to write down some addition and subtraction questions for him to solve, and Sandra wanted me to read to her so that she could memorize the text and then read it for herself. Robbie, on the other hand, seemed to get a great deal of intellectual stimulation from the other children with whom he played, and he provided a lot of input into what the members of the little group would be in the drama they would create. He enjoyed being the leader in these situations, and the other children responded well to his direction.

Because Robbie could read, I felt a responsibility to provide both an acknowledgement of this ability and opportunities for him to practise using his skill. However, my attempts to work with him individually during the learning centre time were quite unsuccessful. As I sat with him looking at books and asking him to read to me, I realized how much he didn't want to be reading, and how much he wanted to be back at the blocks, or painting, or dress-up centres. And so, after a few attempts, I set the idea of reading with Robbie aside and, instead, invited him to help me with the reading of the daily chart when we were together as a group and any other print that found its way into the kindergarten and the program.

Robbie taught me a lot about working with young children. I learned that although he was *able* to read, it didn't mean that he necessarily *wanted* to read at school, and that for him, there were lots of other things he would rather be doing. Robbie knew that he could read and the other children couldn't, and he preferred that his ability be accepted and downplayed so that he would not feel singled out or different. It took a while for me to figure this out and once I did, and just let him be, he seemed a lot happier. However, when several of the other children began to read and were requesting time to read with me or with a parent volunteer, Robbie was quick to take part too. Having others in the group who were able to read was comfortable for Robbie. Being the only one, was not.

In every kindergarten there will be children like Peter, Sandra, Cindy, or Robbie—children who are advanced academically, often because of home circumstances, and for whom, perhaps, additional challenges need to be built into the program. From my experience, the learning centre time is probably the best time to work with these children.

However, as Robbie taught me, it is better to follow the child's lead rather than to impose on the child an adult interpretation or expectation of what the child needs.

September is almost over. It's been hectic. We've sung, we've printed, we've built and crashed with blocks, we've read together, and we've talked and we've listened. I've made so many misjudgements, particularly in my timing. I still haven't got a working sense of how long to engage the children in various program components, or when to help a child with something and when to stay away and let the child work it through on his or her own. But I've done something right because the children and I have become very close very quickly, and there seems to be a feeling of mutual trust and respect in the environment.

Some of the children have begun to read and they have started word box, or language box, collections, and together we share and guess and learn. Of all the mysteries in school living—learning to read is, for me, the greatest mystery of all. How do the children do it? Sylvia Ashton-Warner is my teacher. It's her book *Teacher* that first aroused my curiosity about beginning reading and made me want to learn more. And what can I say about Janet Heagle? Just the finest teacher I've ever known. (When I first taught Grade 2, Janet was just down the hall teaching Grade 1 and was always ready to answer my many questions about programming and to provide ongoing support and encouragement. Later, in another school, when I was teaching Grade 1 for the first time, Janet was my consultant. Her regular visits to my classroom were always welcomed by the children and me, and our follow-up discussions which focused on her observations of the children and the program provided answers to questions I had and direction for my thinking—particularly in the area of emergent and early reading.) How did she get me so interested, especially in early reading? I guess it was her in-class example that hooked me. Above all else, next to loving to be with children, I love to be with them

in their early journeys in reading. But I must be careful. Kindergarten is not the year for all children to learn to read. Parental pressures to get children reading early must be ignored if it's not the right time for the child to begin. I will not give in.

Every child should begin to read with need.
All kindergarten children do not need to begin.

Language Boxes, a.k.a. Word Boxes, or Reading and Writing Boxes

These were shoe boxes I made available to any child who wanted one. Inside, the child kept a collection of personally selected words, phrases, and sentences that came from books we had read, from songs we had sung, from outside school experiences in which the child had been involved...from any source in the child's life. The common characteristic of all the words, phrases, and sentences was the *personal significance to the child.* For this reason, although some words or phrases could be found in several of the children's boxes, the majority were different from collection to collection because each child requested language that came from personal experience.

At first the children told me what words or phrases they wanted and I printed them for them. But as they began to learn the alphabet and began to print, some of them began to print their own words or phrases; others asked me to write down words and they would copy them.

The children used their language collections for reading (for example, putting words and phrases together to make "bigger thoughts"), writing (copying randomly, categorizing for list making, as a reference for inclusion in poetry and story writing attempts, etc.), and talking (sharing with a partner and discussing meanings and ideas), and as a stimulus for art activities. I based the language box strategy on Sylvia Ashton-Warner's work as she describes it in her book *Teacher* although I modified her strategy to include not only words, but also phrases and sentences.

For more about the use of language or word boxes, see pages 72-4.

We build up to eight children working with language boxes. They are delighted. I am too. I must always remember to make our reading times together positive, comfortable, and above all else—successful. No external rewards for these children. I can save so much money by not having to buy gummed stars, or stamp pads, or smelly stickers. Just encouragement and lots of support. I will not promote failure. The children don't need it. They've already got enough troubles—they want to tie their own shoes but they can't, they want to zipper their own coats but they can't, they want to sing on key but they can't. They want to read **and they can!** They can read pictures and eyes and voices and songs. They're very well on their way.

And so we go home for our last September weekend and it looks as if we're all still happy. But October's another month. Besides orange for our colour centre and Hallowe'en for our party...I wonder what the new month will bring? I can hardly wait to find out!

Our last September day is "yellow day." A note home the day before requests that, if possible, the children wear something yellow; so we all come together looking like sunshine. I've brought yellow suckers for all. We lick them and bite them and chew them. Some of the children save them for later at home. Oh, how I admire their restraint!

Out the door they go at 3:30. Take down everything yellow.

Collect things orange and come in on Sunday afternoon to arrange the new colour display.

Prepare the October calendar on which we can record the dates and make a simple sketch of the weather each day. I can already anticipate the excitement when we begin to talk about Hallowe'en coming.

Hallowe'en's coming, Hallowe'en's coming.
Skeletons will be after you;
Witches, cats, and big black bats,
Ghosts and goblins, too!

Flap, flap, flap go the big black bats,
Oooooooooooooooooooooo!
"Meow, Meow, Meow," say the ugly cats,
Oooooooooooooooooooooooooooo! **BOO!**

The days of October flow along. We still get outside frequently, but the warmth of the September sun is behind us, necessitating jackets. We are looking forward to Thanksgiving coming soon, mostly, I think, because we get a day off. I am very tired and I need a little rest and some time away.

One day we all paint orange. A spot for everyone on the floor—a paintbrush and paint and a large piece of good quality painting paper such as manilla tag for all. Dip and create.

Great fun—no spills—**amazing!**

All the four- and five-year-olds, several moms, and Sandra, Joan and I spend an afternoon at the Science Centre. We watch a demonstration of how to recycle paper, and our science consultant comes to the school one afternoon soon after, and works with the children in small groups. Each child makes a piece of recycled paper and takes it home.

Getting a four- or five-year-old to leave something behind at school for display purposes is a real challenge.

"Would you like to put your work up on the wall for everyone to see?"
"No, thank you."
"How about for just one day?"
"No, thank you, I'm taking it home for my mother!"
"Could you bring it back tomorrow to put up?"
"I don't think so!"

The fact that the walls of October in the kindergarten are so bare shows who is winning the battle. I remember my embarrassment on Curriculum Night at the end of September when the parents looked at the huge expanse of bulletin board reserved for the children's work...and there wasn't any because the children insisted on taking everything home!

A lot of singing this month. I remember most of the Hallowe'en songs I taught my Grade 1 children a few years ago and I teach them again this year. Children love Hallowe'en songs and poems and I've got a collection for them.

I made a jack-o'-lantern; I made him yesterday.
I made two eyes like big, round wheels; I made his nose this way.
I made his mouth into a smile With ev'ry tooth in place,
And then a candle lighted up My jack-o'-lantern's face!

During our singing times it amazes me how long the children can sit and watch and listen to me sing without ever feeling the slightest urge to join in!

We spend our days in October much the same as we did in September, but we're all getting so much better at so many things. In particular, I've noticed a real change in the children's desire to sit together in a group more peacefully to listen to a story or to look at something of interest. I think I'm getting better at choosing stories and poems that appeal to four- and five-year-olds and therefore, their interest in the selections is greater. Maybe that has something to do with it. But I also think that as they're coming to know one another better, they're coming to enjoy being with one another more. I've also noticed that there are fewer disagreements among the children while they play and work at the centres. There is more cooperation and collaboration and the children are more able to channel their incredible energy into their play.

As a result of my September and October experiences in the kindergarten, I'm further committed to the belief that children learn best when they make choices for themselves. The physical environment established by the teacher may determine many of the choices that the children can make, but they choose very well from the many alternatives available.

I believe that the only way to get better at doing something is to practise it. And more and more I'm seeing the classroom as a "practise place"—a place where you can try things again and again; where you can take risks without fearing failure. As a result, I have several children who spend long moments practising block building, or painting, or cutting and pasting, or role playing. And daily I am able to observe their demonstrations of progress. I'm glad I believe in letting children make their own choices.

Intrinsic motivation is what I want and there's no better way to develop it than through more open-ended programming. To those parents and teachers who argue that life is filled with deadlines, limits, and "things to be done that we don't want to do" times, I answer that I'm not preparing children for life—they're already in it—and every day is filled with moments that do not catch the attention of every child immediately. Who says that 2:00 each afternoon is when everyone wants to burst into song, or that coming together for a story at any given moment is just right for everyone? But we do it—so the children *are* learning about those times in life too.

About "Sam"

Of all the children in the class, "Sam" provided me with my greatest challenge. His general knowledge and his facility with oral language suggested that he was alert and bright, but his behaviour was unpredictable and often very aggressive. I found myself in such a struggle with him that I had to reach out for assistance to help me to understand him better, and to provide me with more appropriate direction and programming ideas than I was capable of providing for him on my own.

The year started out well for us together. "Sam" was cooperative, pleasant, and industrious. And so, when his behaviour changed, I was surprised. He began to disturb the other children when we were together at The Meeting Place (see page 43). He would interrupt the story as I was reading to the children, and he became physical with the children when things didn't go his way. Rarely did he ever choose to work at centres where he would be working alone and because he frequently chose to work at activities that required interaction and cooperation with other children, for example blocks and dress-up, his inappropriate behaviour became more obvious.

What disturbed me most was that I couldn't find his conscience. When I spoke to him about his behaviour, he just stood absolutely still without revealing any emotion at all. But the aggressive behaviour would resume as soon as he re-engaged in the activity. Early in September, Joan—who had been "Sam's" junior kindergarten teacher the previous year—asked me how he was doing. I replied, "Fine" and our conversation about him ended. By October things were no longer fine, so one day after school I went to Joan and expressed not only my concern, but also my frustration. It was then that she filled me in on her experiences with "Sam." She told me of the very difficult year that they had spent together and she said that the situation had not improved as the year progressed. She had wondered whether there might have been a personality clash between the two of them, and for that reason she decided to give him a fresh start rather than keeping him on her class list for senior kindergarten. She admitted that she could offer me no real help, but she did offer her support when I said that I thought I'd have to seek outside help in dealing with the problem we were having.

I talked the situation over with Eric, my principal, and told him that I was going to have to make direct contact with the home to enlist "Sam's" parents' help. I telephoned his parents and requested that they come to the school to talk with me about "Sam's" progress. We set up a time for a week later, when both his mother and his father could come to the school—and I waited eagerly for that day to arrive.

I was anxious about the interview because it's not easy to tell parents that you are finding it very difficult to work with their child and that you are having little success. And it's not easy for parents to hear that their child is having extreme difficulty at school. But I found that when we sat down together and were able to be forthright with one another without laying any blame in either direction, that the interview became productive. Once we had determined that "Sam" was very difficult to manage at home as well as at school, I asked his parents if they would agree to involving Sheila, the social worker assigned to our school, in helping us to deal with the situation. "Sam's" father said that they would think it over and get back to me.

A few days later they agreed that we should invite Sheila to help us, and with the written permission of the parents, Sheila brought her expertise to the situation. She visited the home several times and conferred with the parents, with "Sam," and with the parents and "Sam" together. On several occasions she visited the kindergarten and observed "Sam" with the other children, and she gave regular and ongoing feedback to the parents and to me. Her suggestions included giving him responsibilities, for example having him help to take out the garbage at home and having him tidy up after himself at school, and then making certain that he carried through with the responsibilities given to him. She also suggested that we should have very specific expectations in terms of his behaviour, and that we must tell him our expectations. She added that the process would take time and that, although we needed to be very firm, we would also need to be very patient.

Sheila continued to be involved throughout the year, and certainly the situation did improve over time. By the end of the year there had been considerable progress—at least to the point that "Sam" and I shared more good days than days of struggle. However, I can't say that I felt successful as "Sam's" kindergarten teacher. Throughout the year I felt a tension between us that shouldn't exist between a teacher and a child. It was "Sam's" aggressive behaviour that, for me, caused my discomfort. However, the support and understanding of his parents combined with Sheila's professional knowledge and objective insights, helped me to work in more positive and consistent ways with "Sam" and to feel a little more comfortable about what I was trying to do to encourage him forward in his development.

It's Hallowe'en! We dress up and parade around the school. All the six-, seven-, eight-, and nine-year-olds join the parade and then we come together in the gym for a big Hallowe'en sing-in.

Three little pumpkins lying very still
In a pumpkin patch on a great big hill.

This one said, "Oh, I'm very, very green;
But I'll be orange on Hallowe'en."

This one said, "Oh me! Oh my!
Today I'll be a pumpkin pie."

This one said, "Oh, I am on my way
To be a Jack-o-lantern gay."

Great fun. Excitement is rampant. An all-time high for the year so far.

We have our party with the lights out and the Hallowe'en jack-o-lantern burning brightly and the children go home—stomachs full—hearts happy.

Big, black cats, Pumpkin faces too,
Staring eyes, Owls are watching you.
Witches riding broomsticks, Past a moon so bright.
'Tis a spooky sight on Hallowe'en night!

The children love to put on impromptu plays or to role-play scenes from books or stories they have read. I must remember to save our Hallowe'en pumpkin so that the children and I can recreate "Peter Peter Pumpkin Eater."

The excitement of Hallowe'en is so quickly behind and bleak November comes to us. What colour should we have? Because the weather is so gloomy, grey or black would be the best choice if we're honest. But instead I choose green to signal the beginning of the festive season. This month is highlighted by the world-famous Metropolitan Toronto Santa Claus Parade.

Get out those seasonal songs and the storehouse of chime-in poetry I've collected to share with the children. Take the children out to see the autumn colours and the signs of winter approaching. No sunshine, no birds. Just leaves of orange, red, and yellow falling to the ground.

"Come away" sang the river to the leaves on the tree
"Let me take you on a journey, for the world you must see."

So the leaves gently falling from the trees on the shore
Sailed away down the river to return nevermore.

Author Unknown

No, no, November, you can't make us sad.
Dark days and cold days can only make us glad.
For we remember when the November days are gone,
Christmas is coming so we'll be happy all the day long.

"No, No, November" from *Play Songs for Children* by Claire Senior Burke,
© Copyright 1951 by Gordon V. Thompson Music, A Division of
Warner/Chappell Music Canada Ltd.,Toronto, Canada.
Reprinted by kind permission.

We spend our "outside" time in the gym now. Just put out all sorts of equipment—balls, bean bags, hoops, ropes, upside-down benches, floor hockey sticks—outline for the children the area for playing floor hockey, and after discussing with them how to use the equipment properly and reminding them to play safely, I just say, *"Go to it."* They all do with such commitment and enthusiasm. Creative movement audiotapes focus attention on listening, body awareness, and coordination. I try the music a few times but the children don't enjoy the restrictions of the tapes. They'd rather move about creatively on their own with the equipment, so I put the tapes away for a while.

I spend my time moving around the gym watching the children, noting their incredible industry, and responding with direct assistance when needed. And frequently I ask myself, *"How come they never get scared in the gym until they get to the top of the rope...well out of my reach?"* (For more about time in the gym, see pages 62-3 and 123-5.)

Responsive Teaching

This is the direct teaching I did in response to something I saw a child doing, heard a child saying, or that a child told me through his/her actions. Responsive teaching is usually unplanned because it happens quite spontaneously. Responsive teaching can also occur when the children are together in a group and a child responds to a question or makes a comment that takes you and the group in a direction that you had not planned. I found this happened frequently following a story that I had read to the children. In the course of the discussion that followed, a child would say something in response to the story and we would end up talking about things I couldn't have imagined! Often the direction in which the children would go would lead to the setting up of a Special Centre in response to their interest or would serve as a focus for continued discussion on subsequent days.

I found that gym times also provided wonderful opportunities for responsive teaching—for example, Robert who wanted to be able to skip rope just needed me to call out *"Jump, jump, jump"* and to applaud his efforts; Robbie welcomed my hand as security when he walked along the overturned bench.

Since the third week in September Joan, Sandra and I have been making use of Grades 5 and 6 pupils to help us with preparation and clean-up. The paste and paints are among the many little chores that require regular attention—*how does white glue know how to get so hard so quickly?!*

Through a newsletter early in the year, we asked parents to indicate if they would be willing to participate in the kindergarten program on a voluntary basis. The response to our request was quite overwhelming. We now feel that it is time to call on our parent volunteers. Our science consultant has termed the kindergarten program as being "very ambitious" because of the many learning centres and opportunities we have made available for the children. Because we are offering the children such a wide range of experiences, the three of us recognize that if our program is to be successful we need more large hands and minds than we three alone can offer.

We contact a nearby senior citizens' home to find out whether there might be any residents there who would like to help us in the kindergarten. We are delighted to find out that there are three who would like to help out on a regular, weekly basis. We arrange for someone from the school to pick them up each week and to take them back at the end of the school day.

We invite the parents who have expressed an interest and willingness to help and the three senior citizens to join us at the school for a meeting over coffee and doughnuts. Together, Joan, Sandra and I outline what we would like them to do, work out time schedules with them, and generally get to know one another a little better. It is the first time any of us have embarked on a volunteer program and we would grow to be very pleased with the results. The extensive learning opportunities we provided for the children throughout the year would never have been possible if it weren't for the kind, interested participation of the volunteers, each of whom visited once a week. (For more about Volunteers, see pages 96-100.)

So that the volunteers will both feel and be productive, I prepare a personal note that welcomes each of the two volunteers who come to help with my group each day, and outline what will (I hope!) be happening during that afternoon. For the first while, I am very specific about the tasks they should undertake to help us out; eventually, as the volunteers become more accustomed to the routines and the flow of the program, point form is all that is necessary.

```
                                                        Tuesday


Dear Mrs. Smith,


Thanks for joining us today. Please keep an eye on the paints and the
cut-and-paste centre. The children are using a lot of materials (espe-
cially red and green!) and these materials may need replenishing
throughout the afternoon. I've cut up the vegetables for the snack.
Would you please put them on plates so they're ready for 2:15. Robbie
says that he needs to read to you and there is a small group of chil-
dren who are sewing and need help threading their needles. We'll be go-
ing to the gym at 2:30 to practise for the concert (please join us, if
you wish), and four children have signed up to work at the Special Ta-
ble when we return. Please give them any assistance they might need.
    As always it will be a busy day here. Thanks for coming in to
help us.
```

The gloomy days of November weather-wise are brightened by these moms, the senior citizens, and yes, on occasion, the dads who join with us. The children are introduced to off-loom weaving, are read to in a one-to-one situation, and are able to count on their snacks every day. A request for one fruit brought in by each child each Monday—the contributions to be pooled for the week—has taught the children and me a great deal about the social graces, for example, sitting quietly, waiting for one's turn, saying "thank you" to the server, as well as providing nourishment at 2:20 each afternoon. Snack time also gives us an opportunity for a quiet time in the middle of our afternoons together. The relatively quiet time is music to my ears! When I combine the food that is brought in by many of the children and that which I contribute, there is always so much that no child ever has to go without. In fact some of the children are delighted when I frequently ask, *"Would anyone care for more?"*

November is also the month I introduce Beethoven to the children. While they model with Plasticene, together we listen to the master and enjoy him. Chopin also finds his way into the program via the nimble fingers of Artur Rubenstein. Young ears listen while fingers model with enthusiasm.

We're all set for the colourful and exciting annual Santa Claus Parade being held in downtown Toronto on Sunday. On Monday we make a big parade mural with crayons. The children colour with enthusiasm and we get a look at the whole parade when we're finished.

There's "Blinky the Talking Car" at the beginning and the jolly man himself at the end.

"That's a great reindeer, Stephanie!"

Our school Christmas Concert, which is held on two consecutive nights, is only four weeks away. What will we do? We'd better get prepared. Sandra, Joan and I decide that two nights is too much for these young children (and for us!) so we decide to have our senior kindergarten children participate on the first evening only. We'll sing and recite poems for the audience. Sixty-eight excited youngsters will collect on a big stage together!!

Celebrations/ Festivities

In many schools today, the student population is made up of children from many different ethnic, cultural, and religious backgrounds and the Christmas Concert is but one of several occasions throughout the year designed to celebrate and acknowledge the different faiths and cultural backgrounds of the children in the school. Indeed, even schools whose students come from largely a Christian background now often have a Holiday Concert rather than a Christmas Concert.

As a staff member you can determine the various celebrations and their timing for the coming year. Then singly, in pairs, or in small teams, responsibilities can be divided so that various staff members can assume leadership roles in preparation for each occasion, for example, Ramadan, Passover, Chinese New Year....Parents of various cultural/religious backgrounds could be invited to take part in the preparations and, perhaps, could visit some classrooms to talk about their customs.

For those schools that do have a large Christian population, the parents and children could be invited to the school one evening in December to join in the singing of the music of the Christmas season.

Do we ever work at those songs and poems!

Unfortunately, as we came to realize later, we give so much time to preparing for the concert that the impending evening seems to take over and become the focal point for our program. We begin to devote our gym times to practising for the concert, much to the dismay of the children. We, too, are unhappy with this development because we believe that our gym times are precious—tremendously important. And we dislike having to give them up.

However, our work on the concert does serve to bring the children in the three classes and Joan, Sandra and me closer together. Now I can put names to many of the children from the big room and I get a better chance to watch and learn from Joan and Sandra as they go about their work with children. They are both very bright people with an understanding of children acquired from a lot of professional reading, but even more so from a lot of listening to and watching children go about their work and play. The professionalism that each brings to her work is refreshing and they are wonderful models for me.

We decide to build on this experience of sharing together and to open up the kindergarten program by combining the three rooms and working together with all the children, beginning on the third day in December. December 1 and 2 are Professional Development Days during which we will confer with all the parents and then somehow find the time to rearrange the rooms to accommodate the new organization we wish to try. If things don't work out, then after the December holiday, we can close the door, go back to the previous arrangement, and carry on.

Before we can confer with the children's families, report cards must be written. Twenty-two stories about twenty-two fascinating people. The children are delightful. They all have idiosyncracies that make each an individual: some are very focused, very attentive; others are very verbal, while others are very quiet; some of the children are more demanding than others, but that's how they get attention, that's how they maintain their individuality. The children accommodate me and my personality and idiosyncracies, so I must be sure to accommodate theirs.

I set out on what I find always an exciting challenge and adventure. Nightly I take the report cards home, sit, and look at the expanse of blankness in front of me. This term at my school the report cards are completely anecdotal so the decision about what to say is entirely my own. I am in control of the content. What will I say—what should I say—what needs to be said?

"...Robbie can read..." The parents already know that. Why tell them?

...more sitting and staring.

Finally I take to my writing. I find it relatively easy once I get started. The children for the most part seem to have adjusted well to the kindergarten and my pen starts creating feverishly once it hits the page. Many words and several evenings later I'm finished. I've re-read each report several times in the process; now I read all of them again. I'm pleased. I've told my stories honestly and with enthusiasm. I've been hampered by a lack of space so the writing is very small and difficult to read in spots.

I get my report cards back with a very kind comment from Eric. During the afternoon I talk briefly with each child about some of the comments I've written on the report card so the child won't be concerned. Then I pack the report cards up in the appropriate envelopes along with a conference sheet inviting each parent to the school for an interview, and I send both home with the children. Now I have only to wait until the parent-teacher interview days for the next hurdle.

Meanwhile in the kindergarten we continue to sing, to paint, to colour with crayons, to print, to read and to listen to stories. And we delight in the first snowfalls of the season.

Funny little snowman, Round and fat,
With your eyes of coal and your stovepipe hat!

Funny little snowman Smiles all day
When the wind is cold and the skies are gray.

Funny little snowman See the sun,
Quick, little snowman! Oh, run, run, run.

The young readers are continuing to explore the world of print and I'm delighting in being a part of their adventure. A few of the children are enjoying the challenge of using their language cards to compose and print their own phrases and sentences to read to me. I take dictation from some of the children and for those who prefer, I use their language cards to compose phrases and sentences for them to read to me. Some of these children experiment with copying their dictation or my "composition." But the real pleasure for all seems to be in illustrating the meaning that comes from the print.

The block builders are constructing higher buildings now and are doing so with greater dexterity. The children at the house centre demand cards to wear around their necks so we know just who they are. Ian loves CAT and he wears his sign with pride. I am finding that the role I play as "teacher" is constantly changing as I move from situation to situation, and from child to child. Sometimes the children ask for specific information or assistance and so I play the more conventional role. But on more occasions and in more situations I find that the children want me to play the role of companion to their learning, and I am being chosen as a regular partner for a game of checkers or Snakes and Ladders. It's an interesting role and I'm sure that, in time, I'll get used to it!

The children's artistic skills are delightful and every day the picture makers add greater detail to their creations. Design has become a popular product as the children experiment with colour and balance. Few are entering into the world of realism as yet. I wonder why that is? Maybe when the children try to colour or paint something from their world of experience, it doesn't come out on the paper as they see it in their minds and so, to their way of thinking, it's not acceptable.

About Pascale

Pascale, at five years of age, was the older of two daughters in a French-Canadian family. Her father, a French-speaking employee of the Quebec government, was sent to Ontario for a year to live, study, work, and be immersed in the English language and the English-language culture. Pascale, like her mother, father, and younger sister, spoke only French when she arrived for her first day at school. For me, as her teacher, Pascale provided the challenge that faces teachers in many classrooms—teaching the English-as-second-language learner.

From the first day of school it was obvious to me that Pascale was feeling extremely uncomfortable in the kindergarten room. Many of the other children had been together in junior kindergarten the year before and they knew each other. But what caused her the most discomfort was the fact that we were all communicating in a language that she didn't understand. It was her first school experience, she knew no one, she was in a new home in a new city, and she couldn't interact verbally with us.

My intuition was all I had to go on, and I kept trying to put myself in her shoes, trying to understand how I would feel if I were in a similar circumstance. I resolved that I would do everything I could not to make her feel any less comfortable than she did already, and I would let her try to find her way. I hoped that her actions would provide me with a direction for giving her the kind of support, assistance, and encouragement she needed. However, the "teacher" in me was not completely comfortable with that approach. I felt that I should be doing something more pro-active. And so, on a few occasions during the first weeks of school, I sat down with Pascale and began to label the room for her! "Table, chair, crayon, paper, blocks, piano, door, boy, girl, book, wall, ceiling," and on and on it went as my eyes darted about the room looking for something...anything...that I could identify in one word—or at most, a short phrase. I would say the word while touching or pointing to the object and she would repeat it—or at least try to. The results were, as one might expect, less-than-successful. Pascale became visibly upset when she couldn't remember the words, and I became frustrated because my approach wasn't working. I wanted so much to help her but I was at a stalemate. Finally, I decided that I would forego my one-on-one times with her until I could find a better way.

That decision turned out to be the best thing I could have done for both of us! Pascale continued to engage in the various learning centre opportunities. She particularly enjoyed picture-making with crayons, paints, and cut-and-paste materials. She spent much of her time at those centres and seemed pleased with the results of her involvements. The children were quite happy to talk to her, knowing that her response would probably be, at most, a smile. And I noticed that they began to involve her with their blockbuilding and dress-up activities—activities that for them had a lot of verbal interaction. As the rest of the children chattered away she said nothing, but she seemed pleased to be a part of the social experience.

Pascale's father often brought her to school and would stop in to see me. At first we communicated in French and he was most accommodating and patient as I wrestled to find the words I needed. Very soon, however, he had acquired enough English from his classes that he became eager to practise using the language. And so, we began to talk together using a mix of French and English. He told me that Pascale was very happy at school and that she talked at great length at home about what we were doing and about the other children. I told him that I was concerned because I wasn't doing anything for her in the way of direct instruction in the English language. He did not see a problem and so I relaxed a little.

One day in November, just after we had begun to think about Christmas and to sing some songs of the season, we were gathered at The Meeting Place (see page 43) to talk about Santa Claus. I asked the children a question and for the first time, Pascale's hand went up. I nodded to her and she began to speak—in English! The words poured out as if she'd been saving them all up just for this moment. I must admit that I stared in disbelief. When she had finished speaking, one of the children said, *"Pascale can talk!"* In unison we applauded; Pascale smiled.

It was a magic moment.

From that time on Pascale never looked back and she participated verbally with increasing confidence. In fact, there were several times during the rest of the year as we congregated at The Meeting Place that I had to remind her that it was time to listen!

I learned from the experience that she needed time on her own to hear the language—to get a feel for its sound and rhythm, and to become comfortable with it. And the best way for her to do that was to be with the other children and to watch them and listen to them—to be immersed in the language—without outside pressure to participate verbally.

It's now the end of November. I see tremendous gains made by many children as I look back to September. Jason now talks to me, Cindy touches, and Robbie now seems more willing to take risks even if he might make a mistake. There is a happy feeling in the kindergarten and the group spirit seems to be developing positively.

Because Monday and Tuesday are interview days, the children do not come to school those days. As I say goodbye to the children on Friday I leave them for four consecutive days—the longest time we've been apart since September 4. This lengthier break is good for all of us. We all need a chance to stretch and to reflect, and these days will allow us to do so.

"See you Wednesday!"

Dismantle the green centre and bring on the red!

Monday morning 9:00. Continuous interviewing all day. Very nice people—concerned, interested, honest. We discuss, we laugh, we get to know each other better. I find out a great deal about them and they about me,

and together we share stored information

about the children.

Tremendous fun and very rewarding...but

definitely tiring!

Tomorrow brings the furniture moving and adjustment of the program that will make it possible for all three classes to be together. In a way, I'm giving up my kindergarten room that for three months has been lived in daily by twenty-two youngsters and me. It's kind of sad. But I'm excited too!

We establish what has been my kindergarten room as "the quiet room," soon to be retitled "the yellow room" because quiet isn't any more natural to four- and five-year-olds than it is to me. We move the television, we join our house centres, all the blocks go into the big room, we expand the book centre, we make space where we can.

Although for the rest of the year the three groups of children will be together during the times they are free to choose their own activities and often for films and music, we also feel the need to continue to work with our own groups to sustain a class identity, to ensure a direct relationship with a group of children, to share quiet times, etc.

I keep a Meeting Place in the yellow room where the children in my group will come together at the beginning of each afternoon, sometimes in the middle of the afternoon, and each day before dismissal. Sandra and Joan each has a Meeting Place in the double room where they can meet with their own groups to take attendance, read stories, and at times introduce experiences in which all the kindergarten classes are going to be involved, for example, field trips, "Growing Things" unit, hatching ducks, etc.

Joan, Sandra, and I came to value the blocks of time when the three groups of children were working together. It gave us the opportunity to get to know all the children and, on a regular basis, to work with the whole group, for example, singing, preparing for a film viewing, engaging the children in a dramatic story telling, etc. However, we also continued to enjoy our times with our own groups and found those times valuable for keeping track of a specific group of children, monitoring the children's progress, and collecting information that could be used for reporting purposes.

Go home.

What will the children say when they see their new room? I've told them to expect and look for a change—but I've kept the details a secret!

Tomorrow will tell.

Children are creatures of habit and I guess they will go on being so. My twenty-two seem to stick with the yellow room. Sandra's and Joan's go to the big room. Chris takes the risk; he enjoys the big blocks so much that he must venture through the door into the big space and find them. Robert's off to the house centre to put on my old grey suit. But at first most stay in the yellow room.

They begin to explore cautiously, knowing that what they really want to do is in the other room, but they won't take the risk. Not today...maybe tomorrow. And each day a few more of my group venture into the double room and children from Sandra's and Joan's groups come in to explore the yellow room.

And still we practise our songs and poems for "The Concert." It looks bad—we're very apprehensive, but the children are trying.

"Louder, we can't hear you."

"Softer—you're yelling."

"...where were you standing yesterday?"

We press on...still a few days' grace left—although I begin to question all the time we are giving to this performance and the educational value of the entire process to the children. I must speak to Eric about this situation and see if we can make some changes for next year.

Right now we're more concerned with getting the macaroni to stick when we glue it on inverted cone-shaped cups.

"My macaroni won't stick."

"Where's mine? I left it here yesterday."

And then when the glue finally dries, Sandra stays after school and sprays all the cones gold. Sixty-eight trees, many nameless, line the window ledges.

This is the first time that we have engaged the children in a craft activity in which they all create the same product and I'm sure it will be the last. It's obvious from the results that we aren't tapping into the children's creative talents and that the process is more an exercise in perseverance than a learning experience. Putting out materials and letting the children investigate and experiment with them would seem to be a more productive and more educationally enriching opportunity for the children.

It's a busy season and the children are very excited. Staff party this Saturday evening and concert night next Tuesday.

The staff party goes very well on Saturday; the dress rehearsal goes very poorly on Monday. The children on the stage wave at their brothers and sisters who make up their audience. They forget to sing and they ignore Sandra, Joan, and me as we frantically exaggerate the motions of frustrated conductors. But we know that a poor dress rehearsal means a good performance.

We go home happy...it was terrible! We should be great!

The auditorium is jammed. Many have to stand. I'm sure every kindergarten child's parents, grandparents, and uncles and aunts from near and far are here. And they only comprise a small portion of the audience! We're the first performers.

I wonder if Joan and Sandra have the children organized to come down?

How will they look?

Will they be as nervous as I am right now?

I've got another job to do before our performance begins. Eric, on the back balcony, indicates his readiness. We're going to ask the audience to join the junior choir in the singing of "Good King Wenceslas." Be calm. Get out there. Make everyone comfortable. Welcome them. Then drop the bomb. We're all going to sing! I do, they do. First hurdle over. The audience is warm, receptive, filled with the spirit of the season.

Here they come—Joan looks frantic, Sandra confused. The children are all bright and shiny as they bounce into the auditorium and up onto the stage. The curtains open, the audience applauds, but the children don't relax. They remind me of Madame Tussaud's Wax Museum at this moment. I've never seen them this way. As the first conductor of the group for the singing and choral chanting, I go out in front of the children, sit on my chair, smile up at them on the stage. Only some of them smile back. We're ready. I nod to Sandra at the piano and she plays the introduction to "Who Is Coming on Christmas Night?" We sing. The audience applauds enthusiastically. The children are cute but they look so ill at ease up there. The rest of what seems to be a never-ending program is all downhill. Three of the boys decide to ham it up and the audience miscues. They laugh. Several of the boys who are most nervous respond by embellishing their performances. Still the audience laughs. Finally, my function as conductor is over and Joan and Sandra are out in front all alone. The audience is with the children as they recite their poems, but the children are by themselves.

"Soon it will be over," I tell myself.

But it goes on and on and on...!

Finally, to the strains of "Jingle Bells," the children leave and the curtains close.

We did it—with pain—but we did it.

We have our Christmas tree. The children cover it with so many paper chains that we can hardly find the branches. And underneath are the gifts for giving and receiving.

In a note sent home earlier in December we asked that each boy bring a wrapped present labelled "to a boy," and that each girl bring a gift labelled "to a girl." In our note we also requested that the cost of the gift not exceed $3.00. The gifts will be distributed randomly at our party.

And to be sure that every child receives a gift, we've bought and wrapped several extras and tucked them under the tree among all the others—just in case!

Two more days and one party to go.

And what a party it is!

The red and green jello made by the children yesterday is consumed easily and very quickly! We have ice cream and a collection of cookies and cakes for the children to enjoy. We give out the gifts and all the children seem delighted when they rip off the paper to reveal the contents.

The whole primary division assembles in the gym to watch the film of the Metropolitan Toronto Santa Claus Parade.

We sing some seasonal songs.

We get ready for home and holidays.

Everyone is excited.

It's been a busy term. We've done a lot of singing, built with a lot of blocks, painted many pictures, and done a lot of thinking. The New Year holds delightful promise and I'm just as excited about my work now as I was during those first weeks in September.

**Kindergarten is a wonderful place to be and I'm
very glad I'm here. I'm loving it!**

Reflections on the First Term

Perhaps what surprised me most of all about my kindergarten experience during the first term was to find out that what I thought I already knew was, in fact, true. Young children **are** capable of self-directing, and they do it well and for long periods of sustained time. I had anticipated regular sessions with the children sitting by my feet listening intently as I read story after story to them; then for a change of pace we'd sing for a while. Well it wasn't to be. The children were quite willing to enjoy a quick story and song, but then they wanted to be off sampling the learning opportunities that awaited them at the various learning centres. I soon realized that although our group times together were very special and important, they had to be purposeful, engaging, and "punchy." My dreams of laid-back days reading to the children and singing with them were soon shattered by the reality of what four- and five-year-old children are really like, and what they want and need.

The success of the kindergarten seems to centre around the climate of mutual trust and respect that develops between the teacher and children, and among the children. We were all brought together purely by chance, and somehow we had to develop a special rapport quickly so we could build a quality life together in the kindergarten environment.

This is what I tried to do. With some children I found this rapport very quickly; with others it took more time. But we all grew together.

I soon discovered that what the children wanted was for me to be a companion to them in their learning, to support and encourage them by being there, but not to direct them too much. They enjoyed it when I was nearby to answer their questions, to hold up the piece of wood they were using for the mast of the sailboat they were constructing, or to sit in the truck they had built with the blocks and go for a ride "around town." They kept me very involved and engaged in their many undertakings.

Some days seemed to go almost as I'd planned them; other days bore little resemblance to the outline on The Planning Board/Chart (see pages 114-17 for more about using a Planning Board). Some days were noisier than others and on some days it seemed that we were continuously interrupted by the public address system or by someone at the door. There were times when confusion seemed to be the order of the day and other days when no one seemed to have any problems out of the ordinary, no one came to the door, and things moved along in relatively peaceful fashion...well, peaceful for kindergarten!

I was especially interested in watching the children at the various learning centres and observing how they went about their work. What particularly impressed me was how much more interesting their work was and how much more their commitment was when they were left to design their own purposes for their learning and how they would go about it. This was especially noticeable at the art and building centres. The products the children created using junk and blocks were creative and original and far more interesting than anything I could have suggested. When left to shape the learning opportunity on their own the children responded to the challenge as an opportunity; when I posed the challenge, for example *"Can you make/build a...?"*, they saw the activity as a test.

As a teacher I learned so much in four months; however, the program had developed only as quickly as I was able to grow. Together, the children and I shared and explored many avenues of learning, and I had a wonderful time!

❖ The Kindergarten Child's Day

Through their play, their involvement, and their commitment, the children engaged in...

box sculpting　　　　snacking

colouring　　　　　number recognition　cutting

gluing

sand playing　　investigating

being read to

listening　　　counting　　**talking**

self-evaluating

water play　　　　　writing

colouring　　　　　playing　　　numbers

painting

cognitive experiences　cooperating

observing　　**talking**　　reading　　experimenting

collaborating

puzzle solving　　creating　　　games

speaking　　sensing　　　singing

exploring　　number manipulation

viewing　　developing an aesthetic sense　**talking**

moving　　　building...and demolition!

wood working　dramatic playing ...

The Second Term: Happy New Year!!

Teachers need their vacations and this holiday was very special...two full weeks and I needed it! I tried to separate myself from my work as much as possible, with the exception of thank-you notes written to the children for lovely gifts received.

> I won't mail the letters.
> I'll take them to school on the first day.
> The children will enjoy taking them home.
> > They love carrying letters home!

And I did spend one day at the school getting the yellow kindergarten room ready for the children—sharpening a few pencils, mixing paints, replenishing the stock of construction paper. And I moved The Meeting Place closer to the windows in the yellow room because the children and I enjoy keeping an eye on the winter weather. I also collected some new books from the school library to read to the children, as well as more picture books to add to the book corner collection. And I set up January's "white table" with a sign inviting the children to "Please bring in something white."

The Meeting Place

This was a very important area in each of the kindergarten rooms. It was nothing more than a space that was large enough for the children to sit comfortably and to be together. But it was in this space that the children and I shared some wonderful times. We sang, we read stories, we planned, we shared, and we even shared secrets in our Meeting Place. In addition to including an easel in the area to hold our BIG books and chart paper for dictations, I tried to make the area as comfortable and as attractive as possible by bringing into the space cushions, little rocking chairs, plants, and a display table of interesting and sundry articles that might capture the children's interest.

It was in The Meeting Place that our community feeling was begun in September and where it was encouraged and sustained throughout the year. However, while little children, by nature, find it quite natural to play and work alone or in pairs, they find working in large groups more difficult. So I eased the children into The Meeting Place gradually. From the first day of school we practised coming together for short periods of time, but it took several months before the children began to function as a group—to listen to one another (well, a little bit!), and to contribute in a cooperative fashion.

As with the learning centres, I changed the location of The Meeting Place in my kindergarten several times during the year—sometimes near a window, sometimes in a quiet corner—but it was always there...

somewhere!

We're back! The news of the holiday fills the kindergarten on our first day back. But very quickly, seasons past fade into memories and we're once again busy learning through painting, colouring, cutting, building....In a very short time, it feels as though we've never been away. The children adjust back to school routines with apparent ease, and they seem excited to find out what the day holds in store for them.

Joan, Sandra, and I have planned a trip for the three groups to McDonald's for next Monday. The children are anticipating our afternoon with delight. Our new little boy, Arif, who just recently came to our school, is still unsure of himself, so he declines the invitation. I hope he'll join us on our next excursion once he feels more secure.

Joan, Sandra and I ask for parent volunteers to accompany us. The parents are very supportive and the response is tremendous. At 1:15 we troop to the bus and journey just slightly south of the school. Shelley is the manager at the McDonald's we're visiting and he organizes us into three groups. We see how milkshakes are made and where the hamburgers and french fries can be found. The children are hungry. The smell of food is overpowering. My group of children is the last group to eat and are we ever ready to enjoy our hamburgers and orange drinks!

It was a good day and the children and I write a large, cooperative "thank-you" chart to Shelley the next day. The children all sign their names with little hands clenching the big black marker to record the most important word of all—one's own name! Then as the children watch, I fold the chart, put it into a large brown envelope, address the envelope and put a stamp on it, and all twenty-three of us go for a walk to the mailbox and drop our letter into the mailslot. The children, of course, are filled with questions about how the envelope will get to Shelley, so we talk about that all the way back to the school.

Although we spend much of the winter term indoors, we do get out for several winter walks (we especially enjoy these walks *during* a snowfall!), and, with the parents' signed permission, several toboggan trips in the park adjoining our school are built into the program. We have great fun on these days. We roll down the hill, we build snowpeople and snow sculptures, we sing and clap snow songs. Back at school, we paint with white—our January colour—and Joan and Sandra get out the detergent flakes so the children can make snow pictures. We put the pictures up on the wall and, as they fall from the walls, I send them home with the children.

This month we concentrate on helping the children develop skills in the gym. We have climbing apparatus on loan from the Board. When I'm with my group in the gym we talk together about using the equipment safely, helping each other, taking our time and waiting our turn, and then twice a week for the next month we spend half an hour climbing, springing, and shimmying up and down the ropes.

Hanging from horizontal ladders is a favourite time for Stephanie.

Michael climbs the bench on a sixty-degree angle to the wall and he makes it to the top every time! I call him a "daredevil" and he smiles gleefully.

The children are enjoying the gym time so much. I'm pleased. I spend this time moving around the gym observing the children at their work and responding to their calls for assistance.

What particularly impresses me is that very few children seem to attempt more than they feel capable of doing on the equipment. There seems to be a "silent alarm" built into most children that says, "That's high enough!" or "Don't let go until you're on the ground!" and we go accident free for the entire month.

I'm both amazed...and relieved!!

The little group of readers are forging ahead. Language boxes are bulging and new printed language is becoming more spontaneously requested and duplicated by the growing number of writers.

The Today Board is now filled out each day by a willing volunteer.

The Today Board

Today is _____ .

Yesterday was _____ .

Tomorrow will be _____ .

The weather today is _____ , _____

and _____ .

There are _____ boys here today.

There are _____ girls here today.

There are _____ children here to day.

Days of the week | Weather words | Numbers

The Today Board

When the children and I began The Today Board activity at the beginning of the school year and for several weeks following, we completed the sequence orally. It wasn't until I felt that the children had an understanding of words that described the weather, could name the days of the week (not necessarily in order!), and were able to count using 1 to 1 correspondence that I introduced the printed board. For a while we completed the board as a class activity, and then it became an independent activity for one or more children to complete. Later in the day, we would look at the filled-in board and take time to read the sentences and to verify the information. Eventually, filling out The Today Board became another activity for anyone who chose to complete it.

So many children are willing to take risks these days and are moving more freely to different centres with a greater sense of confidence.

Some children are becoming more product-oriented—"*I wonder how many pictures I can finish to take home today?*"

Peter avoids working with the art media. I wonder why? He has so much ability in so many areas, I'm sure he could use the materials with very interesting results. But he's more interested in numbers. He counts ad infinitum, and records and solves equations. His interest in learning to read is obvious. He stands peering over my shoulder as I listen to my group of eight share their language box collections.

"Peter, would you like a language box?"

"No, thank you," and he quickly disappears.

And why not! He's finding his own way into reading through the books we read together, and through his decision to read the charts around the room, the song lyrics, The Planning Board, and the environmental print, for example signs or charts that identify the various centres, titles on bulletin boards, labels on shelves and materials and equipment. He's moving into reading in his own way and time and he seems happy. That's what really counts.

The Science Fair is coming soon. As a staff we've agreed that the whole school will participate. Sandra has a great idea for us in the kindergarten—hatching chicks. Great idea, but we can't find anyone to take the chicks when they crack their shells. Lillian has a spot for ducklings but we can't find any duck eggs. Two weeks later we give up and decide to grow things. A letter home—much to the delight of the children—*"Are you going to write a letter?...Are you going to write a letter?"*....outlines our plans for our "Growing Things" unit. We suggest that the children bring in their own special seeds or clippings, and a margarine container for growing. Sandra compiles a long list of plants and vegetables that the children might bring along.

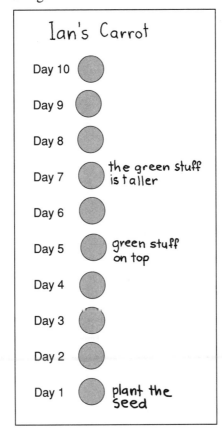

Ian's Carrot

Day 10

Day 9

Day 8

Day 7 — the green stuff is taller

Day 6

Day 5 — green stuff on top

Day 4

Day 3

Day 2

Day 1 — plant the seed

The next day we're inundated with grapefruit seeds, carrots, avocados, radish seeds, cuttings from favourite plants, and beautiful containers to bury the seeds in. When all the seeds are "at home" in their soil, the cuttings are swimming in water, and the avocados are settled in the dark in a cupboard in the kindergarten, I explore record keeping with the children. A long strip of light cardboard and a million gummed circles should do it! Each day we gather together to talk about our plants, to measure any growth, and to discuss any other changes we see. The children attach a circle to their cardboard strip after observing their plants. If anything has happened, we record beside the gummed circles. The circles are numbered daily so a record of days since planting is kept. Some circles fall off and we're picking them out of the rug for days after. But we have learned about record keeping!

Direct Instruction

For a period of some years it has seemed that direct instruction has fallen into disfavour, replaced by leaving the children to explore on their own, or to learn how to do something by "growing into it." To be sure, there are many times when children must be left on their own to discover, or to grow naturally into something. However, there are other times when direct teaching is not only acceptable teaching, but is also responsible teaching. Questions that require a specific answer, directions such as *"Try it this way and then tell me what happens"* or *"Have you thought about...?"* are forms of direct teaching. Of course, we want to be certain that the child is developmentally ready to handle the material or the challenge so that a measure of success will be guaranteed. Therefore, while it is frequently appropriate for the teacher to be the "guide on the side," there are also some times when being the "sage on the stage" is necessary too!

The school's Science Fair evening is a great success. Many of the kindergarten children bring their parents to see their plants growing in the gym. The unit has been successful too—the children are proud.

It's almost February 14th already!

Valentine's Day is a time for giving cards and giving cards and giving cards! I send home a letter along with a class list of first names requesting that if the children would like to bring valentines they bring one for each child on the list. I also talk to the children about why, and their eyes tell me that they understand that if you're left out you'll feel sad.

I cover a big box with pink tissue paper and set up a table with lots of red construction paper and scissors and invite those who wish, to cut out hearts to decorate the box. Everyone wants to take part and soon the box is so covered with hearts of all sizes—and shapes(!)—that the tissue paper can no longer be seen. The children bring in their valentines over the next few days and proudly drop them through the slot. I put one from me for each child in the box, and I store several on which I've printed *"From?"* ready to deliver unobtrusively to those children who might need to receive a few more.

"Have I already given you one?"

"I've lost mine."

"How many did you get?"

Somehow the valentines all get delivered. Hearts come down from the wall for home. Candies and special treats are eaten for the snack today, including a special heart cake made at school by the children yesterday.

"Red and white make pink." Cindy makes this discovery at our colour centre and soon this sentence, printed by Cindy, finds its way into her language box and into her mind, stored forever.

Jacquie and Cindy spend many moments together recording in their scrapbooks—pictures, words, phrases, and sometimes even sentences of importance—sharing and learning together. Robbie reads from an anthology but tires after one page—too much work left to do in the block centre! And so the children grow and experiment and discover, and most of all they are learning to cooperate and to work together.

March brings report-card writing time once more, only this time we have to put in the checkmarks from which we were spared in November. The writing in the anecdotal space moves easily, but the checkmarks are difficult. All are making progress—will an empty box without a checkmark indicate this to those at home? Lots of children take a little longer...and what about the girls who are chronologically almost a year older than some of the boys—how can I compare children?

On the Professional Activity Day, I interview parents who have requested a conference and those with whom I think a conference at this time will be beneficial. The parents are very supportive and they leave me with the feeling that their children are happy in the kindergarten. Joan and Sandra are getting the same feedback...apparently we're being successful!

We continue to create, to share, to talk and to listen—looking forward to the winter break.

Wendy can skip! Hooray!!

Ian can balance along four upturned benches! Hooray!!

A Very Discriminating Activity!

To help the children understand more about colours, sizes and shapes, I gathered the children around a collection of Attribute Blocks that I had put out on the floor. I then talked about various words for shapes, sizes, colours, and thicknesses that could be used to describe the blocks, using words such as "triangle, square, rectangle, large, small, thick, thin."
I then asked if anyone could find:

   (first)   . . . a *triangle*

   (then)   . . . a *red triangle*

   (later)   . . . a *small, red triangle*

   (eventually) . . . a *small, thin, red triangle*

I used this learning strategy on several occasions throughout the year with the children. Each time, leading up to the activity, I would first talk about one attribute only to ensure understanding on the part of the children. For example, I might start with colour. *"Who can find a shape that is blue?"* On the next occasion, I might isolate shape as the distinguishing feature. *"Who can find a square?"* Then I might combine the two attributes, for example, *"Who can find a blue square? A red triangle?"* And so forth.

This experience gave the children an opportunity to consolidate their knowledge about size, colour, shape, and relative thickness, and the chance to store several attributes together in their minds—
   not always an easy thing to do!!

It's March break—time for a week away! A long term—a busy one—a tiring one—a good one. How will our last months flow?

                                    . . . I wonder!

Reflections on the Second Term

This was a productive term both for the children and for me. It was tiring, and at times I must admit, I thought it might never end! There sure were a lot of children and there was so little space. The days were sometimes long—two and a half hours without a stop every day. And although we got outdoors on as many days as possible, the cold weather kept us inside more than during the fall term. And that sometimes made the days feel very long. I wondered how Joan got through five full days a week...every week!

Again this term my children and I learned and we grew.

Pascale acquired so much English we were amazed.

Sandra and I spent a lot of time talking about young children and their learning and about current philosophies and theories that focused on programming for the young. We were both particularly interested in beginning reading and we were searching for the right way to approach the inclusion of a reading component in the kindergarten program. The search was ongoing.

The Final Term: Moving Forward Towards Summer

One day working in the kindergarten during the holidays is enough to get me started for the last term. It's spring and
—*we're going to have recess!*
Snacks for all are gone; outdoors each day at 2:30 is in.

Peter has caught on quickly to reading...he even gets his father to print for him in a scrapbook. During the March break he got his dad to start a language box with him and he just took it from there. His mom reports that he spent his entire spring vacation reading and writing!

With spring approaching, yellow brightens the April room and the happy face remains. We move the piano to a new spot—and a cozier corner for our group to come together results. The volunteers continue to help us out each day. They're a wonderful part of the program.
Kite-making time. And let's look at the pussy willows that are coming in.

I know a little pussy, Her coat is silver gray.
She lives down in the meadow, Not very far away.
Although she is a pussy, She'll never be a cat,
For she's a pussy willow. Now what do you think of that?
Meow, meow, meow, meow, meow, meow, meow, meow!
SCAT!

We're going to hatch ducks. Larry, our Outdoor Education Consultant, has found some duck eggs and has reserved an incubator for us. So we're really going to do it! As long as we get three of the eggs to hatch, we can sing the "Three Little Ducklings" song!

Paddle, paddle, paddle, off they go,
Three little ducklings all in a row.
Paddle, paddle, paddle, Quack, Quack, Quack,
Off to the pond, around and back.

The amaryllis is beautiful—two huge blooms—It only took four months!—*"Thank you, Cindy's mother"*; it was well worth the long wait and the attention.

We're counting by 2s and 10s and we're listening more intently to stories that we've collected from the school library during our weekly timetabled visits there.

The singing is joyful now. March was a bad singing month coming in between winter and spring. But now we will have all the signs of spring to sing about!

Open the windows and Open the doors,
And let the fresh breezes blow in, blow in.
Jack Frost has gone to his home in the North,
And all of a sudden, it's Spring!
Spring, Spring, beautiful Spring,
Hear the good news that the Robins bring.
Old mister Winter, we'll see you again,
But now it's the beautiful Spring.

Paint eggs. Easter is coming. Crunch those egg shells and glue them all over.

Building Together

Some days the children and I would come together for a collaborative building experience. The children would sit around a collection of large and small building blocks that I had put out in random order on the floor in the centre of a large space and I would invite the children, one by one, to contribute to the construction by adding a block of their choice. I encouraged the children to use their imaginations before they added their block by trying to guess what the construction might end up being—*but I asked them to keep their guesses secret!* As various children added their contributions, some of the children had to change their ideas about what the final product might be.

This activity encouraged the children to take turns, to respect the decisions made by others, to use their imaginations, and to alter plans and ideas as they worked their way through the process.

Sometimes, prior to starting, the children and I together decided on the number of blocks we would use on that particular day. This consultation process added another challenge to the experience and a further dimension to the children's thinking.

On some days we come together for a story—often about yellow or spring and we learn to follow along cooperatively. On other occasions, we sing...."Let's Go Fly a Kite" is enjoyed, but our best is "My Grandfather's Clock."

The 1:00 coming together time immediately following the children's entry also provides an opportunity to introduce new activities in the room or for playing cards, rolling big dice, and adding together the numbers that appear by chance.

About Amenda

One Thursday afternoon the children and I were sitting together on the floor in the school library listening as Kathy, our school librarian, read a story to us. Out of the corner of my eye I saw our school secretary, Yvonne, come into the library with a woman and child following. I went over to them and Yvonne introduced me to Amenda and her mother. Amenda's mother smiled; Amenda just looked up at me. Both spoke Japanese; neither spoke English. Fortunately, Kathy was immersed in Japanese culture and customs, and she spoke enough Japanese that she could welcome Amenda and her mother to Canada, to the school, and to the class. Amenda found a place where she could sit down with us and Kathy finished the story and the children then went about choosing books to borrow for home.

I remembered back to my unsuccessful ways of dealing with Pascale, and I decided that with Kathy's help if necessary, I would try to follow Amenda's leads and let her find her way with our support. I asked Sarah, one of the children in the class, if she would be Amenda's partner and help her to find her way around the kindergarten. Sarah took this responsibility very seriously, and soon the partnership turned into a friendship.

Amenda's story unfolded in much the same way as Pascale's had. For about a month, she said nothing. But every day she appeared more confident, and she would choose activities and join with the other children when we came together for a story or singing times.

It was Sarah who, after about a month, came to me to tell me that Amenda could speak English. It was not until a couple of weeks later that Amenda began to communicate with the other children and with me. It appeared that she had decided to trust only Sarah for a while, and once she knew for sure that Sarah understood her, she felt confident enough to let us all in on her amazing accomplishment.

Our regular times at The Meeting Place are really showing results now. The children are functioning more and more as a group—listening to one another, sharing with one another and cooperating together in discussions and activities.

The change in attitude about leaving work for the walls is also very noticeable. No more coercions or battles; the children simply take little pieces of magnetic strip and put their masterpieces up on the wall for everyone to see. The display of their work is left to the children...their choice, their spot, their responsibility. The children are so proud of their work! Now we even have days when we run out of magnetic strips.

I think that in the beginning weeks of kindergarten the children worried that they wouldn't get to take their work home and, therefore, to be sure, they insisted on taking it home that day. Over time, however, they have grown in their trust. They also enjoy seeing their work on display and pointing it out to their friends. Sometimes, however, I wonder how it can be that in this term the children can be so proud of their artwork when they show it to me and point it out to their friends, yet when it's time to take it home they often don't recognize it!

Recess at 2:30—the children love it!

My turn to supervise comes up every third day. Grab a nearby garbage pail and a recycling bin...and out we go. The children seem to run less outside than indoors! (I had learned indoors how wrong I was when I told the children, *"You can't run in the school!!"* They showed me that they could! And they were so delighted that they could hardly wait to turn around to see how proud I was of them.) Now that we are outdoors, many of them just want to hold my hand, arm, or leg(!) and wander around with me. It's pleasant to be outdoors with the children sharing our break together and I enjoy it.

Our school custodian has the hose on today and the children are drawn...mesmerized...like adults to a fire. Most come out when asked or when they are drenched (whichever comes first) but Chris remains. The slow oscillation gives him another thirty-second soaking and then he's off with me behind in pursuit. It takes me a while, but I finally catch up to him...and, although he resists, we make our way back.

Chris seizes many opportunities to test all the adults with whom he comes in contact at school. In situations such as the one described above, no amount of reasoning with him would make a difference to his behaviour. And so, to avoid unnecessary confrontation, I simply took Chris by the hand and explained that we were going back to join the other children who were waiting for us.

By the time we got back to the school, and because it was a warm day, Chris' clothes were quite dry. Otherwise I would have asked him to change into a dry outfit using the clothes that some of the parents had donated to the school for situations like these.

An experience in outdoor living!

The long Easter weekend is upon us. Sandra kindly remembers me and brings me a bag filled with little eggs. We feel the bag and guess.
> *"Marbles"*
> > *"Rocks"*
> > > *"Blocks"*
> *"Reach in—*
> > *take one*
> > > *...you're welcome!"*

Easter bunny's ears are floppy;
Easter bunny's feet are hoppy;
Nose is soft and fur is fluffy;
Tail is short and powder puffy.

Dismantle the walls. Down come the kites. Down come the painted eggs.
Take your pet rock home...

Happy Easter!

We're back. Easter is over, and we're all together again for the final months
in kindergarten living.

"Welcome back, Robbie, from Florida."
"Welcome back, Lisa, from hospital."
"You've both been away for so long. We've missed you."

Now each day as we appear with just a sweater or a jacket, we can collect
quickly around the yellow chair for a few moments together. We sing our
"Good Afternoon" song and then focus in.

Good [afternoon], good [afternoon],
Good [afternoon] to you,
Good [afternoon], good [afternoon],
And how do you do?

Once again I'm amazed by these now five- and-six-year-olds and what
captures their interest, and how able they are to sustain their focus once
they've made a personal commitment to the task. It really makes me wonder
when I hear people talk about children who have a short attention span. It
may be true in some experiences and situations—but then, isn't that true for
all of us? But, for the most part, put a box of Lego in front of a child and then
let's talk about short attention spans!

Nursery Rhymes

Do You Know Why the Dish Ran Away with the Spoon?
Humpty Dumpty sat on a wall,
Humpty Dumpty had a great fall,
All the king's horses and all the king's men
Couldn't put Humpty together again.

Nursery rhymes offer wonderful opportunities for cooperative and collaborative work among children.

I took the children to the staff room to hardboil enough eggs so that each child had one. Each child then created his or her own "Humpty Dumpty." All the children worked together to build a wall using interlocking blocks, and with some Plasticine to secure their eggs to the wall, they created a colourful visual representation of "Humpty Dumpty."

On another day, the children and I visited the staff room with a favourite tart recipe and baked a few dozen tarts for "The Queen of Hearts."

At another time the children in small groups constructed a mobile depicting scenes from "Hey Diddle Diddle."

The children also created a large mural on which they would depict moments from various nursery rhymes as they enjoyed them over a period of time.

As well as providing opportunities for cooperative and collaborative work, these activities also gave the children wonderful opportunities to use their imaginations and to express their creativity.

Sandra has become quite independent about her reading. Her mother says it just happened one weekend..."*I can read,*" said Sandra. And she could! By telephone her mother and I share our amazement and our delight!

I invite Arif to have a language box. He ponders the invitation for twenty-four hours and quietly informs me the next day that he'd like one on Monday. I wonder what he'll choose for his first word? He's been peering over shoulders for awhile now, so he must have a storehouse ready.

Is he a phonics man?

Is he a sight word reader?

How's the visual memory?

And what about configuration?

Questions all waiting to be answered after the weekend. (I might have known—Monday comes and he asks for "house"—and then he adds, "*I can print it by myself*"...and sure enough, he does!)

Interest in numbers is developing nicely. We rote count by 2s and 10s forwards and backwards for fun and for practice, and we can add and subtract a little bit...without even knowing that that's what we're doing!

Getting into Graphing

I found the following activity a fun and easy way to introduce the idea of graphing to the children. For this activity we used an empty egg carton, a dozen little objects each of which fits comfortably into an "egg space," a little bag to hold the objects, and some "yes" and "no" questions. On the

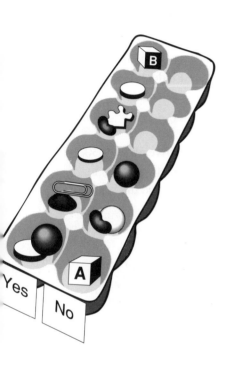

outside of one end of the egg carton at *the end of one row of six,* I printed "yes"; I printed "no" at *the end of the other row of six.* When we began the activity, I selected a "yes/no" question for one of the children to investigate—for example, *"Do you like swimming?"* or *"Do you have a very favourite book?"* Eventually, when several of the children had tried the activity, I invited the children to think of yes/no questions they would like to survey.

After placing the twelve objects in the bag, the child moved around the kindergarten interviewing individual children as they worked at their activities. The child asked the question, and then indicated the response given by taking one of the objects from the bag and putting it into either a "yes" or a "no" space in the egg carton. Sometimes there might be two objects in one space, for example if nine students said yes. When the twelve objects had all been placed in the egg carton, the child knew that the task was completed. Together the child and I then "read" the results—

How many children said "Yes"?

How many children said "No"?

Did more say "Yes" or did more say "No"?

Do more children like swimming or do more children not like swimming?

This activity can be extended by including questions that have a specific answer—for example, *"What is 1 + 1?"* or *"What is the name of our school?"* (Be certain that the child who is going to be asking the question knows the correct answer!) The child then sets out to interview his or her classmates as before; an object placed in a "yes" placeholder indicates a correct response to the question asked.

This approach can be used as an introduction to more complex conventional graphing activities requiring the use of gummed circles, crayons and graph paper, clipboards and tally sheets, etc., by introducing the children to the way that one goes about collecting information for a standard graph and providing information that can be read, as one would read the information on a conventional graph.

The weather is fantastic.

The sun warms...the snow covers!

What's this?—snow at the end of April!

Why did we sing "Frosty the Snowman" for Chris on Friday to make us cool?

Back with the boots and snowsuits and scarves. Getting dressed and undressed reminds me of November but we sure are faster.

Somehow I can't bring myself to set up white paint for snow pictures!

We're going to the zoo, zoo, zoo,
How about you, you, you?
You can come too, too, too,
We're going to the zoo.

Set up the blue table and display panel for May. Rummage around for animal pictures.

Find all of those animal songs from bygone days...really no motivation is needed; the juniors and seniors are excited. All five kindergarten classes are going to the zoo,

all 143 of us!!!

It is a beautiful day.

Letters home request that the children sleep in and arrive about 9:30. Most do wait, but enthusiasm draws about twenty to the door at 9:00. We invite them in. We sing awhile and then get labelled with names and the school phone number and then

away...

rhinos
hippos
elephants   The seal has flaps instead of toes,
snakes   And way up on his tail he goes
birds   To catch a great big strip-ed ball,
bears   And hold it on his nose.
lions...**we   go   !!!**

A happy day.

"What are the shoe boxes for, Mr. Benson?"
"A diorama."
"A what?"

Give them the language and then tell them all about it.

Although much of the kindergarten program is self-directing for the children, there are times when I introduce activities that require certain directions or instructions to help make the process of doing a little easier for the children. This is one of those times. By demonstrating for the children how one might go about creating a diorama, I provide them with a possible way of proceeding. And so, armed with a shoe box, some Plasticine, paint and paint brush, construction paper, scissors and glue, as quickly as possible I show the children the basic steps I follow in creating a diorama. I cut out some rudimentary shapes to represent clouds, trees, and animals. And I talk myself through the task so the children can hear my thinking as I decide where to put each of my cutouts, making certain that the animals are the focal point of the scene I'm creating. When I finish and invite the children to make their own dioramas, I'm a little worried that the children will think they are to copy

what I've done. I needn't have given the possibility a moment's thought...each of the children has his or her own idea...and none of their finished work even slightly resembles my attempt!

Six children attempt to create a zoo inside their shoe boxes. It's hard for little hands to create inside such small boxes, but they do well and we display their dioramas with pride.

Joan and Sandra are more ambitious—papier mâché is the only way to make really big animals:

>   —a huge lion 1 m tall and 2 m long made with big boxes, paste and newspaper...and sticky hands
>   —an artist mother not warned before she arrives that she'll be working with papier mâché...and she has never done so before!

After seeing the bears at the zoo, it seems like the perfect opportunity to clap and chant my way through Michael Rosen and Helen Oxenbury's version of *We're Going on a Bear Hunt,* with the children all ready to join in after the first chorus. They pick up the rhythm and the language in this poem so quickly that soon we're on our feet, making our way through the "long wavy grass" and the "thick oozy mud" complete with actions and sound effects.

Modelling and Demonstrating

Both modelling and demonstrating are powerful teaching strategies. Although many people use the terms interchangeably, I prefer to differentiate, and to think of modelling as *"something we do without explanation,"* and demonstrating as *"modelling with an explanatory component."*

For example, we model for children appropriate ways of behaving in a variety of life situations and settings; we model reading and writing behaviours when we sit down to read or write in view of the children. We also model appropriate ways to hold and use art and writing implements.

Demonstrating, to my way of thinking, adds another dimension, and that is a verbal explanation to accompany the modelling process. For example, when we are showing children how to do something, we can talk our way through the task while the children watch and listen in. The value in demonstrating for the children is that it gives them a possible way to approach a task. The approach you demonstrate may not be the way that all (or any!) children will eventually carry out the task, but it does provide them with a possibility. As some of the kindergarten children move into reading and writing, demonstration becomes a very important and powerful teaching tool, for example re-running a sentence when it doesn't sound right, reminding oneself to capitalize the first word in a written sentence, etc.

Demonstrating is also a very powerful learning tool for children to use. I was reminded of its importance just the other day as I was watching my young son and his friend playing in the swimming pool. Timothy's friend told me that he could hold his breath and touch the bottom of the pool...and then he looked at me and waited for me to say, *"Show me how you do that."* So I did...and he did! And I recognized and remembered how very important it is for us to give children the opportunity to demonstrate for us what they know, what they can do, and what they are in the process of mastering. In the situation cited above it was, of course, impossible for the little boy to describe in words what he was doing as he demonstrated his underwater prowess; however, in the classroom setting not only is it often possible, but it's something that children do quite naturally. They, too, can talk themselves through the task as we listen in.

In the kindergarten, there are many opportunities we can provide for children to demonstrate their learning as they work at the various learning centres. By providing the time for them to show and tell us of their accomplishments, not only can we *see* what they are capable of doing, but also, we get to *hear* the language they use to describe their understandings. Together, this gives us greater insights into what the child can do, how the child performs the task, and the child's linguistic ability to describe the process in which he/she is involved.

It seems that we are continuously moving from one special day to another, with so little time between to relax and catch our breath.

It's Mother's Day on Sunday...long cards with a crayon illustration of mom; a wool hanger and some scratch pad paper stapled on the bottom taken home for the kitchen...with love...for everyone to see.

All the children in my kindergarten live with their mothers, but I must remember when Father's Day comes next month that there are three whose fathers are not in their lives. I'll let them choose someone special they'd like to make a present for when that time comes.

Now at last it's lovely May,
we know the spring has come to stay.
Birdies sing and children play
because it's lovely May.

Dance and sing and play all day,
lovely, lovely, lovely May!
All the world is glad and gay
because it's lovely May.

We love the song, but we don't get to sing it often—May isn't too kind to us this year—more like April.

But we carry on...

We try jumping from a bench on the gym stage into a hoop on a mat below...a long drop for a five-year-old.

Everyone tries while I stand very close by.

"Are you sure you want to try?"...They all do!

No backing out by these kids. Risk-takers—all of them (although I suspect that a few wouldn't have tried if I hadn't been right there close by to keep them safe).

Some are nervous...others brazen.

Everyone lands in the hoop.

Striving for perfection, they all win.

"I think a race looks prettier when everyone comes in even."

The children with language boxes are unbelievable! We've grown to 14!!: Robbie, Sandra, Wendy, Ian, Cindy, Billy, Satish, Michael, Peter, Jacquie, Stephanie, Arif, and the two Sarahs. Each has made personal progress in reading, and all of them seem pleased with their achievements. I am delighted with their interest.

Our handwork has shown wonderful development. A lot of houses are painted and crayoned. I wonder why?...Are they easiest for the children to make, or is home a very special place in their hearts?

Where Is *Your* Native Land?

Today children in kindergarten are often from many different backgrounds. The following activity is one way of helping the children to get to know and understand one another better. By surveying the children's families through a questionnaire to the home, you can develop a list of all the countries represented by the children or their families. Print the information on chart paper with each child's name beside the appropriate country on the list. (Be sure to include yourself!) Count the number of names beside each country and record the totals. This activity also provides an opportunity to show the children how to record in tally form, and to compare numbers that are larger than, smaller than, and equal to.

You might also wish to show the children where each of the countries is located on the globe or on a large map of the world. Although the children will not understand the distances involved, globes and maps seem to hold a fascination for children, and some will enjoy just looking at the globe and map on their own at a later time—perhaps even looking for the country they or their family originally came from.

May is almost over. Already we've experienced nine months together.

Take away May's blue table. Replace it with a table with all the colours—all the bright ones: green, orange, red, yellow, blue. **We'll have a technicolour ending to a technicolour year!!**

We'll have our kindergarten Play Day in June—the juniors and seniors together, with lots of shared activities and lunch following.

So many changes have occurred in the children from September to June—the growth in confidence being the big one. Self-assurance seems a part of almost every child. Most are willing to take risks and try those things with which they have had little or no previous experience. Very little standing on the sidelines now.

More children sing on key now. Music in the kindergarten is certainly not as easy as it looked to me as an outsider. Getting children to participate vocally is not a simple chore. The children were very content to sit and let me sing, but getting in there with one's own voice is a risk and it takes time. They're getting better, but some still need more time.

The children can echo clap with the best of them, however. I've spent considerable time with echo clapping. We develop listening, observation, cooperation, and coordination through the activity and it gets the children actively involved.

Likewise with the gym program. Coordination has definitely improved for so many through their active involvement. The gym time has been a highlight for me and I have come to enjoy and value these times so much. The children are very happy and are actively participating. Learning through physical activity is tremendous:

responsibility		throwing
decision making	leaning	

cooperation		skipping
body movement	catching	standing
body awareness		jumping
dancing		pushing
observing	chasing	pulling
listening		
running		direction changing
		stopping

See pages 123-5 for more about activities and learning in the gym.

We've read, we've printed, we've counted, we've painted...cut...pasted...ripped...sung...listened...talked...shared...fought...loved.

Every day, the one time never missed has been clean-up. Some days not everyone might sing, visit the library or the gym, or paint, but everyone always has to clean up!!

...a focal point!!

Why is it that whenever I say *"Tidy up"* every child is able to find something else to do that he or she says is *"very important"*? How does one make clean up an intriguing, exciting experience? I think—no, I know—I failed at this!

Lights out as a signal.

Everyone stops, looks and listens.

The same instruction—

> *"Boys and girls, it's clean-up time."*
> *"Are you helping?"*
> *"Put that here—put that there."*

Sometimes it seems to me that my "commands" are going unnoticed, and yet every day the room somehow gets tidied up and ready for the next day.

The Clean-up Challenge

I tried several different approaches to the task of bringing a bit of variety to clean up, a time that I didn't enjoy any more than the children did...

• I set the kitchen timer for a certain length of time so we could see how much we could clean up in a minute, two minutes...whatever seemed appropriate for the day.

• Sometimes I'd count out loud to an agreed-upon number.

• On some days I'd ask the children to guess how far I'd have to count before the room would be ready. (They loved to see if they could guess that one!)

• Some days I'd ask the girls to clean up for the first minute and the boys for the next minute. The next day we'd reverse the order.

• Another approach I used was to ask the children to pick up and put away three things, or 2 + 3 things, or 5 - 2 things, or something red, something blue, something that is your favourite colour, something round, something square, something rectangular in shape.

> • I tried playing a familiar song on the piano and the children had to stop when it finished. Other times the children would clean up until the piano music stopped; then they were to freeze until the music started again.
>
> I tried just about everything I could think of to bring a little fun to what is a routine, but very necessary daily undertaking. I knew the difficulty was that the children couldn't understand the purpose for having to clean up and so, for them, it was a rather meaningless exercise. As the year went along, I must admit that they did get faster. However, it never became a time towards which the children or I looked forward!

It's been a big year, a fun year, a learning year, a growing year...for the children and for me.

I'm glad I had the experience.

Next year there will be two Grade 1 classes and a combined Grades 1 and 2 class, but not enough kindergarten children for me to stay as a kindergarten teacher, so I'm going to go with the children into and through their Grade 1 year.

I'm excited about that!

Looking Back on That Wonderful Year

Although I was only able to get a grasp on kindergarten, I enjoyed it tremendously. What a wonderful teaching and learning opportunity it was!

I guess more than anything else I learned about programming for the very young that year was that programming for kindergarten is not all that different from good program design for older children. Some of the learning experiences are different, and the depth of exploration into some topics is different. But interestingly enough, I found more similarities than differences when I compared teaching kindergarten to teaching the grades.

However, the differences were **so** different! What a wonderful eye-opener!

Teaching kindergarten is not easy. Kindergarteners are very active and there is always a lot happening at any given moment. The children delight in doing, and they need a lot of time and opportunity to move and to become involved in their work. You find yourself in perpetual motion. There is so much to be doing! And it's constant—until the spring there's no recess break to catch your breath, no times when you can move back and away from the group.

You're on all the time!!

In fact, I was so busy all the time that by the end of the day although the children's energy was still high, I often needed to sit down and relax for a few minutes.

Everything we do with children in kindergarten has the inherent spirit of play associated with it. Children have already learned to play, and as they play they learn. And there is such spontaneity associated with all the learning experiences—even when they are carefully pre-planned! I have to admit that as I set out on a learning adventure with the children, I often had little idea where the children might take me...or where we might end up!

However, to say that the kindergarten program is play-based is not to say that the children didn't work hard and think hard while at their play—they certainly did! In fact, it was their strong commitment to working hard and thinking hard that initially caught me a little off guard. I had expected that I would have to do much more for them than was actually the case. But four- and five-year-olds are quite happy to do for themselves.

So over time I learned that my primary role was to frame the children's experiences, and then to let the children shape their own learning. My job, the children taught me, was to create a varied, stimulating, and challenging learning environment filled with all sorts of meaningful, appropriate, and participatory learning opportunities, and then to stay out of the children's way and let them show me what they could do.

I also discovered that the time children spend in kindergarten is vitally important time. They learn so much!! Indeed, as author Robert Fulghum writes: "Most of what I really need to know about how to live and what to do and how to be I learned in kindergarten" (see page 128 for some of Fulghum's kindergarten learnings).

❖ And Where Do We Go From Here?

Teaching kindergarten is never complete without considering what's next, what's ahead. At the end of my year in the kindergarten I found myself thinking about Grade 1 for my group of kindergarten children—not in terms of *"Are they ready?"* or *"Have I prepared them?"* for this is not my job. But rather, I looked ahead to where they must go. I knew that the children didn't need a permanent desk and chair, a pencil of their own, or day-long quiet and sitting. And some, I knew, were going to find the challenge of a full day at school quite difficult. (A visit to almost any Grade 1 class during any afternoon in September reminds us of this. There are always a few children who have their heads down on a table, or are curled up in a corner...fast asleep! And in the staff room, Grade 1 teachers often talk about the children who forget to return in the afternoon, who ask at morning recess, *"Is it lunch time?"* or who at afternoon recess head straight for home!)

September, as I see it, is a fresh start—a new classroom and a new school life. We must, however, preserve the kindergarten in the children's lives. Like the grades, kindergarten is a ten-month experience, and so much is learned that is reflected in the children's eyes and talk and pictures. The value of the kindergarten program and the enthusiasm of the children must travel forward into and through the grades.

Why not a Grade 1 classroom with tables and chairs and no desks, and a cubbyhole or bin for personal belongings?

Why not...

- blocks and sand and water

- a house centre and nails and hammers?

Who says these materials are good for kindergarten but not for Grade 1?

If we truly believe in growth for individuals then we **must** have such materials—there really is no alternative because many of our kindergartners are not yet finished building and hammering and dressing up. Some have just made a start.

And what is more soothing for anyone than water? Sand makes big castles and hills...and long roads and trails. Maybe the children could measure them and compare them. Lego pieces can be counted, sorted, attached. Snakes and Ladders can be played with two die—they can add!

The September- and October- and November- and December-borns especially need more time. What better way to provide this time than by offering them an environment with which they are familiar and in which they feel comfortable?

The reading will come—it did in the kindergarten...and so will numbers, geometry, and measurement.

The journey from kindergarten to Grade 1 is long and there's a wide bridge to cross. If we hurry the children across that bridge too quickly, their chances of success will be greatly diminished. We must help the children to cross carefully and make sure they all get safely to the other side. We must be patient and give the children every opportunity to be successful at school. If we believe in childhood, then we will.

❖ Some Closing Thoughts

There is so much more to be shared about teaching and learning in the kindergarten than the space in this book allows. As you have been reading through the story of my year in the kindergarten, each of you who has taught or is currently teaching kindergarten has probably written another book in your mind. As you've read about one situation I experienced, you've probably thought about five others that have happened to you. And when you read about the learning centres you probably mentally added others such as modelling, cooking, woodworking, and a quiet centre to the list. Our Christmas Concert has probably conjured up in your mind many of the "very well-rehearsed but somehow they never got quite polished times"...as the parents watched in!

For those in teacher education programs and those early in their teaching careers, I hope that you have been able to capture how delightful and how very special teaching kindergarten can be. And I hope that very soon you will have your own stories to tell.

**The stories of kindergarten are important...
they ARE the beginnings!**

Little children reach out
Receive them...accept them
Tell them not what they should be, but rather,
Find out who each is.
Let them grow;
Give guidance
Encourage their smiles...you smile too
Learn from them
Young
Impressionable
Looking up
      Get down
            And be with them
Growing and learning together...
      ...with care.

                    R.B.

Part III:

Thinking About Learning and Teaching in the Kindergarten

The nature of the child must determine
all the details of his [her] education, and an
educational institution must be so
organized as to afford room for adaptation
to the inclination and needs of the
individual pupil.
— *Johann Pestalozzi*

To render experience into words is the real
business of schools.
— *James Moffett*

In every human being...there lies
and lives humanity as a whole, but
in each one it is realized and
expressed in a wholly particular,
peculiar, personal, unique
manner.
— *Friedrich Froebel*

Knowledge begins
in experience...
— *Johann Pestalozzi*

The classroom should be a rich learning environment deliberately designed with much to
explore, to wonder about, and to get active with.
— *Erik Erikson*

There is no doubt that the children's days in the kindergarten are very busy. From the large-group sessions for singing and dancing, being read to, gym time, planning together, and sharing in talks about important things, through the small-group times when a few of the children gathered together to focus on something that interested them or to work on a project together, to the personal learning times when each child explored and investigated something of personal interest—there was little time out for any child...or for me!

**Learning for all of us just never stopped
from the first "hello" to the last "goodbye"!**

Although I was thinking primarily of new and in-training-to-be kindergarten teachers as I wrote the material in Parts III and IV of Beginnings, *I also very much hope that those of you who have been teaching kindergarten for some time will find something of value, something of interest to you as well.*

Language and Language Development in the Kindergarten

Listening to talk is hearing a child's mind at work.
—*John McInnes*

Because language is central to learning, the common element in all the children's learning experiences in the kindergarten will be language—the language the child brings to the experience and the language the child takes away. Therefore it is vitally important that as we plan our kindergarten programs and organize the learning environment, we pay attention to the possibilities for language development, with particular consideration being given to providing as many opportunities as possible for the children to **talk.** The kindergarten year(s) is an opportune time for children to consolidate their already phenomenal oral language mastery, and to experiment with and extend their verbal prowess. And so, although the kindergarten is often noisy with the sounds of children talking, there is a need for it to be that way...and it should be encouraged.

As well, with the growing numbers of children whose first language is not English, it is important to include as many opportunities for the children not only to hear the English language, but also for them to practise using it in an open, non-threatening environment. This means that there must be large blocks of time during which talk is not only permitted—it is encouraged, accepted, and expected! Only through such opportunities will these children become more comfortable with the language and use it with greater ease.

Because there seems to be some confusion around the meaning of the term "whole language," I prefer, when I think about language experiences for children, to think in terms of "authentic" or "natural" (rather than contrived) ways of engaging the children in learning opportunities that both encourage and extend their language capabilities. The learning centres provide these opportunities in so many ways. There are centres that encourage—and yes, even **demand**—talk, and those that tap into opportunities for listening, writing, reading, and viewing. And integrated participatory experiences in science, social studies, mathematics, drama, physical education, visual arts, music...are the vehicles for language acquisition and usage. Through involvement and interactions with others—other children, volunteers, and teachers—the children constantly add new vocabulary to their repertoire.

Always I tried to capture those situations that could be used as meaningful ways of leading into and connecting reading and writing. Some learning centres offer ideal opportunities for the children to begin to read and write in natural and authentic ways. For example, in the housekeeping centre, we can provide long narrow slips of paper by the "fridge" on which the children can write lists of groceries. We can make sure that there is a notepad by the telephone where the children can leave messages for one another. If our classroom includes a hospital centre, we can make sure that we provide prescription pads, X-ray sheets and other types of material that allow for context-specific writing and reading events.

❖ From Writing to Reading...From Reading to Writing

It's natural for children to want to make their mark on their world. Reading and writing allow them to do just that and it became apparent to me very early in the year that it is impossible to separate reading from writing —and undoubtedly a mistake even to try!

To facilitate the children's ease into reading and writing, I filled the classroom with print. For example, as well as making sure that the classroom contained lots of books that would appeal to the children, I devised as many opportunities as possible for the children to become acquainted with environmental print:

> • **names that identify** children in the class, days of the week
>
> • **labels that locate** various toys, games, classroom learning centres and materials
>
> • **signs that inform and direct behaviour,** both inside the kindergarten and the school and beyond the school walls: for example, EXIT, STOP, OFFICE,...McDONALD'S (Is there a child anywhere in North America who doesn't recognize this sign?)

Through their various experiences with environmental print, the children came to learn some of the special functions of written language, and some began to show an interest in acquiring a collection of names, labels, and signs that they could read. Some wanted to print their own labels and signs and use them in particular locations and situations to suit their particular purposes. I also posted around the room the children's writings, the lyrics to the songs we learned, the recipes for our many cooking experiences (both the successful and the not-so-successful!), and lists of books we read together.

The children's dictations, which I or an adult volunteer took down from the children and printed on charts for them, provided yet another opportunity for the children to look at print, to examine its surface features, and to grow in their understanding of the many purposes that print serves. Some of these dictations were taken from the children individually; others were recorded on charts in the group setting. These opportunities allowed me to comment on, as I wrote, such writing conventions as *"Start at the top left,"* and mechanics such as *"Begin with a capital/upper case letter."* As well, the children were learning that what you could think about, you could talk about, and what you could talk about, you could write about and then read. We displayed most of our group dictations, and we kept the personal dictations that the children didn't wish to take home in a collection held together by a large ring so that we could add to the collection regularly and easily.

The group charts resulted from a whole-class experience (for example, a field trip, a response to a book we'd read together) and served as a means of reflecting on the experience and recording group impressions. Developing these group dictation charts was not something I did every day with the children, but rather, the children and I did them together on those occasions when it seemed to make sense to record information or impressions that the children might want or need to refer to at a later time. Some of the children liked to take a group-developed chart and copy some of the words or sentences from it.

Individual dictations were taken on request and I would try to use these one-on-one opportunities to find out what individual children knew about writing and reading. Depending on the child, I would ask questions such as *"Where should I start to write?" "What kind of letter should I start with?" "Do you know how that word starts?" "I'm at the end of the line so where should I write the next word?"* I tried very hard to ensure that the children did not feel that dictation time was a test time. Nevertheless, I did find that these individual dictations and the group dictations were very useful times for me to discover who was learning what about writing and reading.

All the children in my kindergarten were given the opportunity to play with their name cards (the cards I gave them on the first day with their names printed on them—see pages 14 and 80-1 for more about name cards), to look at the print in the books I read to them, to read the lyrics to the songs we had learned, to participate in the creation of the group charts and to dictate a personal sentence, paragraph, or story for me to record. However, in my particular kindergarten I had a number of children whose interest in reading and writing went further than that. For these children in particular, I found the use of word boxes or language boxes (see also page 23) an invaluable tool in providing them with an extension to their growing understanding of print and its conventions and purposes. These boxes were simply empty shoe boxes I brought to school into which the children could put cards on which I had printed, at the child's suggestion, words, phrases and sentences that had personal meaning for that particular child.

Robbie started us off. He could already read words and sentences and stories, although he often preferred to work with blocks and swings and ropes and crayons. Because I was learning about reading and writing in the kindergarten, and because Robbie could already read and write, I used him as my teacher. I decided that before I started a language box with any of the other children, I would let Robbie give me some clues and directions about how to handle this component of the program. As well, I re-read Sylvia Ashton-Warner's *Teacher* to re-acquaint myself with how she worked with children's organic vocabulary as a way of engaging the children in meaning-ful, personal reading experiences. The major difference I decided to make was to try to elicit *sentences* from the children that I could print for them rather than the *single-word* approach that Ashton-Warner had used.

Robbie was a great teacher for me because he had no trouble creating sentences that had personal significance to him, and he was often able to take the thin marking pen from my hand and print some of the words for himself, spelling the words aloud as he printed them! These few times I spent with Robbie gave me an opportunity to learn about and to practise how I would frame the language-box experience for other children who were ready to use the boxes: *to let the child talk first as a way of creating the eventual sentence that we would record; the questions to ask to promote the talk; how much writing I should do and how much the child should do; and to be sensitive to the length of time we spent together so that the child wouldn't become disin-terested and overly anxious to return to other activities.* During our few times together, perhaps Robbie didn't learn much more about reading and writing than he already knew, but he did help me to organize in my mind a way to introduce the procedure to other interested children—and Sandra, for one, was waiting anxiously on the sidelines; she just needed to be invited to start her language box.

When children who asked for a language box offered a single word only for me to record, I would ask them if they could put the word in a sen-tence. If they could, I would print the sentence on the back of the card; if not, that was okay because the child had made the choice of word—it had per-sonal significance—and the child already had a context for the word that had come out in the talk time.

Eight children requested language boxes early in the year. I began the language box with each child individually. By doing so, I could find out what each child knew about literacy conventions, the ease with which the child was moving into reading and writing, and the degree of personal com-mitment that the child was making to learning to read or write. This kind of knowledge better enabled me to find the role I was to play. With some it was more the role of guide, while with others more direction was appropriate. Once I had a sense of where each child was along the interest and develop-mental continuum, I began to bring the group of eight beginning readers to-gether on occasion so they could interact, compare, and play with their collections.

Every day at first to establish the routine—then a few times a week—we would add a sentence, a phrase, or a word to the collections. I kept a record of the children's choices...just a scrapbook with a few pages set aside for each child.

It wasn't long before Cindy—who had accumulated several single-word cards—discovered that by putting two words together she could create a "silly phrase" and she could hardly wait to show me what she had done! *"pumpkin Cindy"* was her first discovery. I couldn't have imagined how quickly she would spread the word around the kindergarten! That seemed to start the other children who had single-word collections in their language boxes to do the same thing, and soon these youngsters were asking for sentence cards. And many of the children wanted "silly sentences"—*"Cindy is a pumpkin." "Sandra has orange shoes."*

The children enjoyed making illustrations of the sentences, phrases, and words they had accumulated. They discovered that if they could read them, they could illustrate them, and then I knew that they were making sense of the print. Always at the front of my mind was to be sure that the children **were constructing meaning.**

And if we laughed when we wrote and read our funny sentences, then we really understood.

"Robbie's mother is a train."

Some days we rhymed words and printed them...Marianne, Sandra, Ian and Sarah were good at this. On other days we sorted and classified in a variety of ways.... *"Please find **l o n g** words, short words, **people** words, colour words, size words, all shape words"."* *Can you find words that start with the letter...s?"* (Cindy didn't like this last request very much or anything that even remotely involved phonics. She and phonics rarely met. She used some other method and had great success with it.)

Because outside pressures to teach children how to read and write at the kindergarten level were not that strong (although these pressures seem to be increasing)—the pressures I did feel were very much self-based!—I found that I could be more relaxed in my explorations with the children of the writing and reading processes. My difficulty was learning to be patient when a child showed an interest in reading and/or writing and not to rush the child, but to follow the cues and clues the children gave me by providing an appropriate environment and suitable conditions for them to explore and discover what they wanted and needed to know about language.

*As the year progressed, the children came to discover that when we needed to **know** something, we often went to books;*
*when we wanted to **remember** something, we often turned to writing.*

Writing in the Kindergarten

To make it easier for any child who wanted to experiment with writing, I made sure that there were a variety of unlined and lined paper of differing shapes, sizes and colours, and an assortment of writing tools and surfaces such as pencils, magic markers, chalk, crayons, magic slates, and portable chalkboards readily available at a number of the learning centres. I also introduced unlined scrapbooks and writer's folders into which the children could gather all their writing, and I put a few of each on a table at the writing

centre for anyone to choose. The children who did choose to do their writing in a scrapbook or to collect their writings into folders gave me an excellent opportunity to observe both the process and the progress of their writing over time.

Whatever surface and tool the children selected for their writing, it was interesting to observe the range of activity that resulted. Some children recorded any words that came to mind—words that to me seemed completely unrelated; other children attempted to create sentences using their own invented spellings; some copied words from the available dictionaries or the word lists that we had developed together that related to the topics of our discussions; some printed letters of the alphabet; some practised printing the words and phrases they had gathered in their language boxes; and some were inspired by the stories I read to them and tried to capture some of their reflections by recording the names of characters, titles, or words that had some kind of personal significance, sounded nice, or were new to them.

I found that through talking about writing and through my demonstrations—for example, taking personal and group dictations from the children, printing the lyrics to the songs we were learning, printing the poems we enjoyed—many of the children started to build understandings about writing, and several began to use pencil, marker, or crayon on paper to see what would happen. Several of the children attempted and delighted in printing their names, and many made signs to accompany projects they were working on—*"John's twr"* (John's tower) or *"Chris ma dit"* (Chris made it).

We all know that as adults we go about our writing in a variety of ways. We also all realize that writing is a sensitive activity because it is so very personal. So I worked hard to refrain from directing the children and chose, as best I could, to respond in the direction of how the child was going about his or her writing, offering suggestions whenever it seemed appropriate to do so.

I tried to offer assistance to the children with the more mechanistic aspects of their writing as a way of helping to make what is, without question, a very hard process, just a little bit easier: for example, reminding the child who was confused, of the "left-to-right-return-left" convention; suggesting paper with a baseline when I thought that might help the child to keep a sense of direction, or to bring a degree of uniformity to the size of the letters; suggesting that the child try a different-sized pencil that might make the grasp and control of the implement a little easier. I was constantly reminded, as I watched the children trying to connect tool to surface, of how much is involved—especially for the young child—in the physical aspect of the writing process, and of how important it is to do whatever we can to make the experience a little bit easier and a little more pleasant.

When a child appeared ready, or in need, I would draw a baseline for the child on the unlined paper, and eventually, in some cases, I drew another line to indicate an appropriate height. (I never did figure out a name for that line!) The "top line" helped some children to increase the size of the letters; for others it helped them to shrink the letters. However, most of the children who chose to begin writing on unlined paper, continued to prefer to use the unlined page!

Several of the children, over the course of the year, did venture into keeping a scrapbook or folder of original writing—recording thoughts and ideas that they wished to keep as a permanent record (the beginning of a response journal!—a response to something they had read or experienced: a story; an event in their lives; something significant they wanted to remember and recall later). It was at this time that I got to see the range of writing development—from the wavy line scribble through the appearance of some recognizable letters (often the initial and sometimes final consonants of the words being represented), to collections of letters with spaces between, and in some cases phrases and whole sentences, and in a few instances a whole paragraph! It was also at this time that the children introduced me to what I call "temporary spelling" (also known as invented/inventive/natural/ developmental spelling). I prefer to call the kindergarten child's spelling **temporary**

- because it is!
- because I found that parents felt more comfortable knowing that these unconventional spellings wouldn't last forever!

Most of all, as children started their tentative voyages into the world of writing, I tried to offer support and encouragement as a way of sustaining the child's interest in pursuing writing as a worthwhile activity. Unlike reading, where the author has already created the words to form the ideas, writing requires and reveals so much of oneself in the creating process that I felt that more than anything else, *the children needed to be supported in their writing, and that acceptance of what they were doing was paramount.*

Reading in the Kindergarten

The intent of the reading component in the kindergarten program should be

- to promote the development of positive attitudes towards print

and

- to enable children to have confidence in their ability to learn to read

Reading is a part of human life and definitely a part of school life. The big question is—*when should the young child begin to read?* What a difficult question to answer! If it is true that children will become frustrated and discouraged if we move them into reading too early—that is, before they themselves are ready to read—then we must respond with sensitivity when they do show an early interest. Because there has been, and I venture to guess that there always will be, a continuing debate surrounding the place of learning to read in kindergarten, I decided that it is important to talk about my experiences with reading as I worked with my particular group of four- and five-year-olds.

I do not want to give the impression that I believe kindergarten is the year when children should be focused on learning to read. Yet through my experience as a kindergarten teacher, I quickly came to realize that there may be children who come to kindergarten already reading, and others who come from homes where they have been read to regularly, where reading is highly valued, and where they see people engaged in reading as a regular and natural part of their daily lives. Such a background often piques the child's curiosity to such a degree that the child looks to us to sustain this intrinsic, self-motivated interest by providing opportunities that will support his or her growth towards becoming a reader.

Within my group, a number of the children showed a keen interest in unlocking the mysteries of the reading process. I must admit that this situation was not something I had expected to be dealing with in the kindergarten, and so I began the year quite unprepared for the challenge that lay ahead. But all of a sudden I was faced with a boy who could already read, and a few who showed a very strong, personal interest in beginning—children who were on the brink! I knew I had to acknowledge this interest and respond to it in a responsible way.

I gave the situation a lot of thought during the first weeks of school because I wanted to make certain that learning to read didn't become **the** focal point of the program for **any** of the children. I wanted the children to realize that in kindergarten, reading is no more important than block building or painting or dress-up. It may be a part of the kindergarten day for some, but never any more a part than are all the other appealing activities that are available.

As a former Grade 1 teacher, I was aware that many of the six-year-olds I had taught were not ready to be engaged in a formal reading program until later in the Grade 1 year (and some even later than that!). And here I was facing a group of youngsters who were chronologically at least a year younger! However, as when I was with the Grade 1 children, I recognized that I was working with youngsters who brought a range of abilities, experiences, interests, and talents with them to the kindergarten, and I saw it as my job and my responsibility to incorporate and use these as the foundation for the kindergarten program—including the reading component.

Earlier in my teaching career I had been greatly influenced by Sylvia Ashton-Warner's work as described in her book *Teacher* and by the work of

Dr. Russell Stauffer in *The Language-Experience Approach to the Teaching of Reading* (2nd edition). I identified strongly with these authors' belief that reading is very personal and that the more closely we, as teachers, can integrate early reading experiences with the child's personal life experiences, interests, and knowledge of language and how it works, the better the chance of success. I also believed that children could have success reading "real" books, that it was important for the children to look at books, to learn how book language goes, to have the opportunity to handle books and practise reading behaviours, to develop a story sense, and to experience a close, personal, and positive association with print.

I believe that for most children, learning to read can be an easy process. The difficulty, I think, is that unintentionally, we can somehow give children the idea that reading is difficult. Because we must ensure that the child *prefers* **to** *read,* rather than *prefers* **not** *to read,* it is important that we allow those children who do wish to begin, to ease themselves into reading comfortably, and that we follow their leads. Opportunities that enable the children to extend their love of books and to increase their confidence in dealing with printed language both in books and in their environment are important in helping the children to grow into reading naturally and comfortably.

All children when they begin to read must do so with feelings of success. For this reason, I would not expect most children to learn to read during their kindergarten year(s). In fact, there will be some groups of kindergarten children that come along in which there is no one who shows an interest in reading beyond being read to and looking at the pictures in books. And that, I believe, is just fine. Young children need time to engage in other enriching experiences. For those children in my group who did show an interest in learning to read, I found that the availability of a variety of pattern,

predictable, and BIG books, the experience of being read to, access to the stories and poems I had read to the class, the collection of lyrics to the songs we had learned, the classroom labels and signs, and the availability of language boxes seemed to satisfy their needs.

And I don't think that the importance of reading to the children can ever be overstated! Reading to children regularly and frequently, looking at and enjoying the illustrations, talking about words, telling and retelling stories, and immersing children in a language-rich environment seems to me to be the best approach for kindergarten and Grade 1 teachers to use when introducing the young child to the world of print.

By being read to, the children are given opportunities

• to hear the language of print and to distinguish it from spoken language

• to relate illustrations to print

• to listen to expressive reading

• to respond to the rhythm and sounds of book language.

In today's multi-ethnic, multi-cultural kindergartens, we have the added opportunity to enrich the kindergarten program by reading stories to the children that bring the variety of cultural backgrounds of the children to the classroom. Not only does such a practice acknowledge the diversity of cultures represented by the children, but also, the delight in the children's eyes as they hear stories that originated in their country of birth or that of their parents will go far in helping those children to know they are truly accepted and valued in the kindergarten.

Finally, we must also ensure that *all* children are involved in an ongoing reading of pictures, ideas, block structures, and displays. For isn't reading being able to construct meaning? If children cannot make sense of their world, they will have difficulty making meaning from print. This relationship necessitates a very verbal, highly interactive program for young children. We must listen to what the children are saying so we can know whether they are able to construct meaning from their environment before we begin even to think of easing them into the abstract, vicarious world of print.

And so, the personal language of the children, the frequent reading to the children, and the regular and ongoing associations with a variety of books and other print materials available in the kindergarten became our entry point into the exciting world of learning to read—for those who wanted to begin.

For our first day together in September, I had prepared name cards, hand-printed with magic marker, and I used these cards as a way of taking attendance, for seeing which children already recognized their names, and as a way for me to match name to child. It was on this first day that I realized how much the children enjoyed seeing their names in print, and so, as the number of children who recognized their own names and the names of the other children increased, I began to use the name cards in a variety of ways. On some days I would have all the name cards out on tables, chairs, bookshelves—anywhere I could find a spot, and the children would find their own and put it in the "I am here today" envelope beneath The Today Board (see page 46 for more about The Today Board). On other days, as the children came into the kindergarten, I would hand them a card at random and they would have to match the name on the card to the right child, and then give it to the child who would then put it in the envelope. Sometimes as we were going through the cards to take attendance, we would look for names that started with the same letter and we would say the names to see if we could hear that they started with the same sound. We also used the name cards as a way to learn the letter names, and the children started to notice such things as, *"Robbie and Peter both have 'e's in their names"* and *"Cindy and Peter both have five letters in their names."* I also used the name cards to help the children distinguish between a letter and a word—something I knew confused a lot of beginning readers and that needed to be sorted out early. Because the children took such an interest in their name cards and in playing with them, I used the cards in as many ways as I could think of to expose the children to some of the surface features of print.

From the first day of kindergarten, I made it a point to read to the children twice a day—once shortly after their arrival, and again just before they left for home. This routine continued throughout the year, and it proved to be the way of entry into reading for several of the children.

In September, the read-to times were just that—the children and I gathered together at The Meeting Place (see page 43 for more about The Meeting Place) and I read stories and poems to the children. As the year progressed, I began to engage the children more and more in looking at the print and following along as I read to them. And then we would revisit the text and look at and talk about some of the words, the sentences, and the conventions of printed language. BIG BOOKS were especially good for this purpose. It was interesting, as I read to the children, to watch and note those children whose eyes were following the print, those who were more focused on the illustrations, and those who weren't looking at either!

Re-reading several of the children's favourites allowed the children to commit the stories to memory so they could "read" along with me. *Brown Bear, Brown Bear, What Do You See?* and *Mrs. Wishy-Washy* were two of several favourites, and in no time at all the children were able to read both of them! I came to realize how very important it was to include in the reading-to times, books that could be easily memorized by the children and that contained bright and simple illustrations so the children could read the pictures to read the text. It was also important to read books that would give the children new information on topics of interest, and those that dealt with value issues so we could talk about *"What would you do if...?"*

As the children became more comfortable with books and with talking about them I would often engage them in talking about the story before I read it to them—what did they think the story might be about, how did they think the story might go, what did they think might happen, and so forth. And sometimes we would talk about the story first as a way of building a schema for dealing with and better understanding the story content. Often, however, we would just plunge right in! Following the reading we might talk briefly about the story, and I used this opportunity to find out what the story had meant to individual children and how well they had seemed to understand it. Sometimes we would talk about some of the words the author had used; other times we would recall some of the content. Regularly I asked the children if they had enjoyed the story or poem and why. And certainly, whenever possible I encouraged the children to join in and read along with me.

My purpose while reading to the children was not to teach them how to read or to involve them in a formal reading program, but rather to expose them to the world of print, to book language, to get them thinking and talking about stories, poetry, and books, and, of course, to engage and heighten their interest in print!

There are many wonderful books available to read to young children. A few of my favourites are *The Camel Who Took a Walk* by Jack Tworkov, *The Turnip* adapted by June Melser, *Chicka Chicka Boom Boom* by Bill Martin, Jr., *Thump Thump Rat-aTat-Tat* by Gene Baer, *The Teeny Tiny Woman* retold by Barbara Seuling, *Ira Sleeps Over* by Bernard Waber, *Carousel* by Donald Crews, *Shake My Sillies Out* and *Everything Grows* in the Raffi *Songs to Read* collection, *Twenty-four Robbers* by Audrey Wood, *Hot Pursuit* by Kees Moerbeek and Carla Dijs, *There Were Ten in the Bed* (traditional song) illustrated by Pam Adams, anything written and/or illustrated by Brian Wildsmith, anything written or adapted by Bill Martin, Jr., and all the books recommended by the school librarian!

Another regular component of our reading time was to sing the songs we had learned as we "read" the lyrics that I had printed on chart paper for the children. If the song was a short one, I would print the lyrics as the children dictated them to me; however, usually I had them printed on chart paper and hanging on the flipchart for the children's reference. The printed song lyrics gave me an opportunity to point out the way that rhyming poetry is organized when it's written down, and together we would look for rhyming words and examine the similarities and differences.

The environmental print in the classroom provided us with another opportunity to look at and talk about print. Above each centre I printed a large sign to identify the location of materials and activities, for example: *"You can look at books here." "This is the cut-and-paste centre." "The blocks are here." "This is The Meeting Place."* I suspended the signs from the ceiling with enough butcher cord so that the signs would hang low enough for the children to see them, and regularly throughout the year I would change the wording on the signs; for example, *"Come here to build with blocks." "You can read here."* We also had signs that said *"in"* and *"out"* (for washroom purposes, as we didn't have a washroom in our kindergarten), *"exit,"* and labels for some of the equipment in the classroom, for example, *"piano," "easel."*

As a result of my experience in the kindergarten, I've decided that readiness for reading, simply stated, is **wanting to learn to read.** Some of the children in my kindergarten asked, *"Can I have a language box?"* Others said, *"Can I learn how to read now please!"* It was almost as if, somehow, the children knew for themselves that the time was right!

Because I didn't get to all my readers as frequently as I would have liked to, many of them began to print their own words, phrases, and sentences on the available cards—going to one another for help rather than waiting for me. I began to think that maybe we don't teach children how to read, but rather, that our role as teacher is to provide the environment and opportunities for children to learn to read. And I learned that that role is an important one—*to create an environment that promotes literacy, and to respond to, encourage, and support those children who show an interest in learning to read.*

The Buddy Program

Beginning in the second term and continuing through to the end of the school year, the kindergarten children met with a buddy from one of our Grade 6 classes. Because the three kindergarten groups participated, there were more than twice the number of kindergarten children. Therefore, the Grade 6 students had two or three younger buddies. For one-half hour every Tuesday afternoon, the older children came to the kindergarten prepared to talk with and to read to their young partners. Joan, Sandra, and I had met with Les, the teacher of the Grade 6 class that was to be involved, to talk about the purposes and direction for the weekly meetings and to organize the groupings. Regularly throughout the year we continued to meet to make any changes that we saw as necessary.

Although the program began with the Grade 6 children assuming the leadership role—for example, they brought short stories to read to the children as well as topics of interest to discuss—it wasn't long before the younger children wanted to read to their buddies, to show them their paintings and block structures, or to direct the conversation. Of course, the Grade 6 children always had to come prepared—just in case!

We found this program inclusion to be important for several reasons. For the Grade 6 students it provided an opportunity not only to prepare for something very important but also, to assume responsibility for their young charges. It also gave many of them the opportunity to revisit some of their favourite stories and books and to rehearse their reading in preparation for a real audience.

For the kindergarten children, the program became a time to which they could look forward to being read to in a small-group situation and to talk about things they wanted to talk about. Eventually, the time gave some of them the opportunity to read to their older buddies and to share some of their accomplishments.

Once the Tuesday afternoon routine became well established, we introduced some organizational changes. Because there were almost one hundred children involved, we asked the Grade 6 students to meet their buddies in the kindergarten and then, depending on the plans they had made for the time, to move to an appropriate spot in the kindergarten room, the school library, or their Grade 6 classroom. Joan, Sandra, Les, the volunteers, and I used the time to roam through the various areas where the children were working to observe and support.

Towards the end of the year it became possible for the groups to plan ahead for the next week and together the children would agree on what they would do at their next meeting, with some of the groups going together to the library to choose the books for the Grade 6 students to practise in preparation for the following week. Often, at the end of the day, a kindergarten child could be seen taking home the book that his or her buddy had read that day! For several of my group, this shared time with their Grade 6 buddies provided the motivation for wanting to learn to read.

Assessment and Evaluation in the Kindergarten

- **Why** are we evaluating?
- **How** will we collect our information?
- **What** will we do with the results?

These are important questions to consider so that the assessment and evaluation processes are purposeful and useful.

There are several reasons why kindergarten teachers collect information to be used in the evaluation of a child's progress:

- to give feedback to the child
- to certify a "level of achievement"
- to modify the program for the child as appropriate
- to report to parents/guardians on the progress and accomplishments of the child
- to identify the strengths/abilities and "becoming strengths" of the child
- to learn about the child's interests
- to know the child well

Knowing our purposes for collecting information about the children's progress, accomplishments, and achievements helps us to determine not only **what** we will observe, but **how** we can best go about keeping track of the information we collect.

What do kindergarten teachers need to know about assessment and evaluation to be able to provide a comprehensive profile on the children's progress and achievements? This is an important question and one that is not easily answered. There is so much focus on accountability, outcomes and evaluation in education today that sometimes I have the feeling that we are expected to be super experts in the field. Nevertheless, I do think the question of what we need to know about assessment and evaluation is an important one and I'd like to share some of what I learned in my year in the kindergarten and what I am continuing to learn.

	MONITORING	• **what** the child does
and		
	TRACKING	• **how** the child does it

Assessment is the collection—the monitoring and the tracking—of information, and **evaluation** is the judgement we apply to the assessment. Both are important components of the teacher's role, and with the busyness of the kindergarten, neither is easy to accomplish. Therefore, it becomes very important that we make time to move around the kindergarten and look at **what** the child is doing, and **how** the child is doing it. This is often not a planned-for time, but rather something that happens during those moments when the children are busy at their work and things are relatively peaceful.

❖ Assessment

In the kindergarten, the most frequently used assessment technique is observation. **Observation** can be defined as "the storing of impressions from what we see, what we hear, and what we are told." This means that we must spend time **watching** the children, **listening** to the children, and **interacting** with the children. In my kindergarten I developed a "Check In, Check Out, Check Back" model of observation that proved very effective in allowing me to observe the progress of a child or group of children in my kindergarten class.

Check In, Check Out, Check Back

> When I first visited the block centre *(check in)*, I observed that Robbie, Ian, Robert, Peter, Sandra, and Satish had just made the decision to build the tallest building they could. I acknowledged to them my understanding of what I heard them say they were going to do, and I asked if they needed any help. They said, "No," so I watched for a brief time to see who was going to assume what role—the leader, the follower, the builder, the site director, etc.
>
> As soon as I could see they had the construction well organized and on its way, I complimented them on a good start and told them I'd be back in a while to see how they were doing *(check out)*. I then made my way to other centres to observe and interact with other children. A short while later, I returned to the block centre *(check back)*. I observed that "the tall building" was only one block high, and that the blocks travelled over a large amount of floor space in a rather irregular pattern—not the square or rectangular shape that I had expected. When I inquired, I was told that they had decided to make *"a highway with a lot of roads coming out of it so we can race our cars around."*
>
> Checking back let me in on the change of plans as well as giving me an opportunity to see that each child seemed to have assumed a rather equal role in the construction, with no child seeming to be the leader. As well, I was able to observe that this particular group could work both cooperatively and collaboratively.
>
> In other situations the check back gave me the opportunity to provide the children with some verbal, and on occasion, physical assistance, as well as giving me the time to observe the progress being made and the learning strategies being employed.

"What is the child telling me?" is, I believe, a key question for us to keep asking ourselves as we observe.

- When we **watch** a child, we should ask ourselves, *"What is the child telling me?"*
- When we **listen** to a child, we should ask ourselves, *"What is the child telling me?"*
- When we **talk** with a child, we should ask ourselves, *"What is the child telling me?"*

As children interact with their environment, they are giving us messages about **how** they are learning and **what** they are learning. As observers, we need to watch carefully, and to identify the significant incidents so that we may add them to the information we are collecting about each child's progress, achievements, accomplishments, and learning attitudes and styles.

There are several techniques we can use to record information (see pages 90-5). Regardless of what method we use, what is so important to remember is that we need only record the *important* information that we see, hear, or are told—**the significant incidents.** And this is not easy because, potentially, everything is important or appears to have the potential for importance. A way of beginning to discriminate is to make certain that we do not record the same information day after day. For example, if a child prints his/her name for the first time—**this is important—a significant event**. And it should be recorded. If the child does the same thing the next day, it's not necessary to record it again. Now it's time to be looking for something different. However, when the child makes a leap in the way he or she prints his/her name, for example, moving from all upper-case letters to the appropriate use of upper and lower case—this is the time to record that observation to enable us to report on growth over time.

All observations should be dated so that we can see at a glance over what period of time a change—the growth—took place. Some teachers have great success keeping work folders for every child in which samples of significant work are kept. Then they have the actual work to look at when they begin to evaluate for reporting purposes.

- Identifying the important learnings that need to be recorded takes time and practice.
- It is therefore necessary to watch closely, to listen carefully, and to discriminate wisely.

❖ Evaluation

Evaluation requires that decisions about the child's progress and/or achievements be made. Sometimes the decisions lead to program modifications; at other times the decisions are used for reporting purposes.

Currently there are several evaluation techniques in use, and each provides us with a different perspective on children's learning. **Formative** evaluation, **summative** evaluation, **self**-evaluation, and **peer**-evaluation all hold promise for making evaluation a more complete process. And each can be used with success in the kindergarten program.

Formative evaluations occur regularly throughout the learning process. These are the day-to-day judgements that we make as we watch and listen to the children. As we collect information about the child we make professional decisions based on what the child is doing. These decisions often lead to program modifications to ensure both challenge and success for the child.

Summative evaluation occurs at the end of something—the end of a unit, a theme, or in the case of the kindergarten, more usually the end of a painting, a block-building experience, a cut-and-paste, a jigsaw puzzle....And, of course, we must evaluate summatively at the end of the term as we set our impressions on paper for reporting purposes. In the kindergarten, summative evaluation is used to evaluate the end-product that emerges from a learning process in which the child has been involved.

Self-evaluation gives the child the opportunity to respond to what he/she has done. It is important to help the children shape their personal evaluations by framing them through the use of leading questions. Questions such as *"What do you like about...?" "How did you make...?"* can lead the child into revealing a great deal of important information that we can use to understand better the child's attitude, growing knowledge base, and developing skills.

Peer-evaluation is, perhaps, the most difficult form of evaluation. As with self-evaluation, peer-evaluation should be carefully framed for the children. Questions such as *"What do you like best about Peter's painting?"* or *"What do you think is the most interesting part of the castle that Sasha built?"* will serve to keep the comments positive, encouraging, and forward-looking.

*It is extremely important that we think of **all** forms of assessment and evaluation in a **diagnostic** sense. That is, what does the information I'm collecting tell me about the child's progress (formative) and accomplishments (summative), and what could or should I do with the information to assist the child in his or her learning?*

Introducing Peter

I observed Peter working at the math centre. He had elected to work there and had chosen to print myriad numerals on a plain sheet of paper. I observed that regularly he made the numerals 2 and 5 backwards. Recording this information was just the first step. Now I had to decide what, if anything, I should do about it and this was a difficult decision because it required almost in an instant that I reflect on what I knew about Peter—very interested in and curious about mathematics; very self-directing; very eager to learn, yet sometimes curiously reticent about trying new things; seemingly very content at school; very sensitive!

Generally all characteristics directed me towards showing Peter how to form the numerals correctly. But it was the last characteristic—"very sensitive"—that made me hold back momentarily. Finally, I decided that I **would** demonstrate the numeral formations for him, but I approached the situation by first complimenting him on what he was doing, and acknowledging the time and care he was giving to his work. I then commented that there were two numerals he had printed backwards and asked him if he knew which two they were (fully expecting that he wouldn't know or else he wouldn't have reversed them in the first place! But I was grasping a bit and buying myself some time, not wanting to dampen his enthusiasm for what he was doing). He didn't know, so I pointed to the 2 and the 5 and then I printed both on his page as he watched, and I suggested that he might want to refer to them as he worked.

He did, and for the rest of his time at the math centre that day, he made correctly formed 2s and 5s. The next day, however, he reverted back to what he knew and understood.

Diagnostic assessment and evaluation requires that we determine what a child can do, together and in concert with what the child is having difficulty doing, and then determine what to do to help the child. In Peter's case he knew how to print all sorts of numbers—single, and two and three digit—and he could read back any number he had printed. His only difficulty was in forming the numerals 2 and 5. Deciding whether it was important or not for him to be able to form his 2s and 5s correctly was the decision I had to make. I chose to show him and he showed me, by his next-day response, that he wasn't quite ready to assimilate the new information at that time.

By the end of the kindergarten year, through ongoing exposure and regular self-initiated practice times, Peter was able to "correct" his backward 2s and 5s without any further assistance from me.

At the present time I'm thinking a lot about summative evaluation and some of its possible limitations when used in a conventional way. Conventional summative evaluation is like a snapshot—a picture of a child at a particular moment—and so often, that's where it ends—as a mark, a grading, or an anecdotal comment that is stored away for later use on a report card or for discussion at a parent/teacher conference. And the more I think about summative evaluation, the more it seems so final—so terminal! Yet learning isn't like that; learning never stops—even momentarily. And so, the more I think about summative evaluation and the way it is often used, the more I believe there is something missing.

All evaluation should provide us with information, and this information should be used to help us take the child further along the learning continuum. In that way, summative evaluation should not be just an ending, but also a beginning. As I think this through I am trying somehow to combine summative and formative evaluation in such a way that we can evaluate a "product"/a "result," while at the same time we can use the information gathered and the judgement made, to lead the child forward in his or her learning. Perhaps **ongoing-summative evaluation** captures the essence of what I'm thinking about. For example: the kindergarten child finishes a painting, a block structure,...whatever. When the child shares the product with us, I think we need to be looking at and thinking about not only the results of that process, but also, and perhaps more important, about how the results of that experience can take the child further. And then, through our dialogue with the child about the work, we can help the child to move ahead. In this way, this particular experience and what the child has learned from the involvement become the beginning of the next experience the child has when using the same materials. Even the description of an achievement recorded on end-of-year report cards can be written in such a way that it not only identifies the accomplishment, it also contains an indication of the significance of the achievement, and where the accomplishment seems to be taking the child. One way of thinking about it might be, "Because of this accomplishment, then...".

Summative evaluation has its place to be sure, but I do believe its usefulness is significantly increased and extended when it is combined with an **ongoing** component such as we find in formative evaluation. And I think that all evaluation needs to be thought of in that kind of forward-looking way.

❖ Some Tools for Recording Our Observations

There are a variety of methods for recording our observations, and most teachers find it useful to employ a number of these techniques. Some of the more frequently used techniques include the following:

- checklists
- observation guides (lists of behaviours to which an anecdotal response is recorded)
- informal inventories (surveys that can be used to record the children's attitudes towards what they are doing and learning)
- work folders
- pupil profiles
- audio and visual recordings
- conferences
- pupil self-assessment

It would be impossible to use all the techniques identified above at any one time; however, using a variety of assessment techniques provides us with a more eclectic portrait of the child's progress and achievements.

CHECKLISTS: Checklists are one of the best ways of recording information quickly, and they can be used successfully in developing a profile of the child's progress and learning styles. Not only can we collect information quickly using checklists, we can also easily retrieve the information.

One way we can use a checklist is to track pupil behaviours. When designing such a checklist it is first necessary to decide what behaviours we want to observe. Some of these behaviours can be drawn from the headings on our report cards; others will be those that out of personal interest we want to know more about and that we want to observe in the children.

With checklists it's always a good idea to include space for brief anecdotal comments that relate to the checklist behaviours being observed. This

Behaviours Checklist

NAMES	BEHAVIOURS TO OBSERVE	ANECDOTAL COMMENTS
Peter	Social interactions	– very gregarious – friendly towards all
Ian	social interactions	– somewhat shy – kind – helpful to others
Cindy	Social interactions	– very quiet/soft spoken – interacts directly only with Jacquie
Sarah B.	perserverence at centres	– needs frequent and regular reassurance

allows us to explain or embellish our checklist observations and to provide additional information that could be very useful at report card and parent/guardian interview times.

We can also use checklists to keep a running record of the various learning strategies the children use as they go about their work in the kindergarten.

Because we know that children learn in a variety of ways, it is important that we identify each child's natural ways of learning and then provide learning opportunities through which the child can use those learning strategies with which he/she is most comfortable. A checklist such as the one on page 92 can provide us with interesting information related to the individual child's learning. Over time we may see patterns emerging for each child, for example, the child who engages regularly in activities that require talking or listening or first-hand experiences. Keeping a running record of the learning strategies used by the child can sometimes be a real eye-opener.

To make productive use of a learning strategies checklist I developed to use with my children, I attached the checklist to a clipboard and, as I moved around the kindergarten, I put checkmarks under the child's name in the boxes that described the learning strategy(ies) the child was using to do his/her work.

For example, when I observed Sandra working with others at the block centre, I noted that she was **showing** the other children how to place the blocks so they wouldn't topple over, **telling** the others what to do next, **problem solving** when trying to decide where to put the next block, **demonstrating** evidence of an understanding of the need for patterning by building a row using the same block shapes to provide reinforcement for the structure, and **listening** to the ideas of the other children.

Because one observation does not make a pattern, I made a point of observing Sandra again at the block centre—check in, check out, check back—and at several centres in the kindergarten to see if she employed these learning strategies on a frequent and a regular basis. For this reason, I made sure that the boxes on my checklist were large enough that I could put several indicators in the same box—both as a frequency tally and, eventually, as evidence of a pattern.

Learning Strategies Checklist

LEARNING STRATEGIES	JOHN	SASHA	MARTA	...
INVESTIGATING	✔ ✔	✔		'
PRACTISING			✔ ✔	
EXPLORING	✔			
TELLING		✔ ✔		
DEMONSTRATING	✔		✔	
SHARING	✔ ✔ ✔		✔	
LISTENING	✔ ✔ *very attentive, learns a lot of information from listening*	✔	✔	
SPEAKING				
PROBLEM SOLVING	✔ ✔	✔		
EVALUATING		✔ ✔ ✔	✔	
ROLE PLAYING	✔			
MANIPULATING		✔ ✔	✔	
OBSERVING				
CONSTRUCTING	✔	✔	✔	
REPORTING	*likes to talk about accomplishments*			
CLASSIFYING			✔ ✔	
MEMORIZING				
PATTERNING	✔ ✔	✔ ✔	✔ ✔ ✔	
QUESTIONING		✔ ✔ *very inquisitive about everything*		
DRAWING	✔		✔ ✔	

WORK FOLDERS: A kindergarten child's work folder is not unlike an artist's portfolio!! In fact, much of the work we collect will be the artwork of the child. We should make sure that any work put into the folder is dated so that we can look at the children's growth over time. When possible and appropriate, the children should make some decisions about the work they would like to put into their folders.

The children's folders need to be stored somewhere. Some teachers have found that record stands or very sturdy boxes are well suited for storage purposes. If classroom space allows, it can be advantageous to store the folders in a place that permits the children access to their folders. This access frees us from always having to put the work in each child's folder ourselves.

The materials in the children's folders can be used when writing formal evaluations and also when meeting with the children's parents/guardians.

AUDIO RECORDINGS: There are at least two ways in which this technique can be used to gather information. One method, and the most frequently used, is, with permission of the children, to turn on the tape recorder when conferring with a child or small group of children. Later you can replay the tape and listen to the conversation, noting the language usage of the child or children, vocabulary, the purposes for which the child or children use language, intonation and expression, etc.

Another method is to place a tape recorder near a highly verbal/interactive centre. Although when we listen to the tape later we may not be able to distinguish individual voices, we will be able to get a general sense of the language being used by the children and the ways in which the children verbally interact at the particular centre. (Initially when we try this technique, the children may be somewhat inhibited by the presence of the tape recorder, but very soon they will forget about it and will carry on as if it weren't there!)

VIDEO RECORDINGS: This can be an exciting and valuable technique for gathering important information about the children. In addition to **hearing** the children, we **see** them **"in action"**! Once the children become used to the intrusion of the camcorder, they will ignore its presence and carry on. It may take a little while for this to happen, so it will probably be necessary to exercise some patience! (The children will be thrilled to watch themselves and, of course, they should be given the opportunity to do so.)

PHOTOGRAPHS/SLIDES: Although we lose the movement and "progress in action" that we are able to capture with video recordings, the study of a photograph or slide of a child can be very revealing and informative. Often, minute details can be observed that are sometimes missed when we are viewing movement—for example, noting the way the child holds a writing or art implement; a moment of surprise or astonishment when the child makes a discovery; what the eyes of the child tell us at a particular moment. And of course, the fact that a photograph is readily accessible at any time for study and examination is certainly a plus. The photographs can be kept in an album for sharing at parent/guardian interview time as well as for viewing and enjoyment by the children.

CONFERENCES: Talking one-on-one with a child is probably the most valuable and important way to collect information about that child. Not only can we learn about the child's growing information base, but also we can capture first-hand how the child is feeling about him/herself as a learner and as a person. Such conferences should be designed to ensure that all children have the opportunity to talk with us—something every child should enjoy. We might ask the child to bring to the conference a piece of work of his, her, or our choice, for example, a painting, a Plasticene model, etc. Or it may be that we hold the conference around the block structure that the child has created or the part of the mural the child has painted. And sometimes a conference will involve several children who have been working together on a collaborative project.

The questions we ask should be designed to elicit information from the children, for example: *"What are you working on?"* (if what you are asking about is a work-in-progress), *"What have you made?" "How did you think of the idea?" "How did you make this part?" "How did you make this unusual colour?" "What do you like best about what you've done?" "How does it work?"*, etc., etc. Of course, we need to focus the conference on only a couple of questions—we need to be careful not to belabour our questions or the child will tire of the interrogation!—and the questions should focus specifically on the particular project in which the child is involved and should serve to draw out what the child wants to tell us. A good question to ask prior to the closing of the conference is, *"Is there anything else you want to tell me about your work?"*

As teachers, we should be sure to remember to thank the children for their information and to offer our support through an encouraging, closing comment.

SELF-ASSESSMENT/SELF-EVALUATION: Young children are very capable self-evaluators. They love to talk about their play and to tell us what they are doing. Careful teacher-questioning can draw out important information about what the child is learning through the experience and his/her feelings and emotions regarding the undertaking. Self-evaluation must be carefully framed for the child so that the focus for the information we are seeking can be elicited. Of course, we need to leave the framing sufficiently flexible so that we may go in whatever directions that the child's responsive talk may take us. This journey can be so exciting and such a learning opportunity for teachers of the young.

The questions that we ask during a self-assessment/self-evaluation time are often similar to those we might ask during a child-teacher conference; however, the focus should always include what the child wants to tell us as well as what we want to know and therefore will be more of the *"Did you enjoy making this?"* and *"Why?"* variety. At report card and interview time, many teachers are finding success with questions such as *"What do you enjoy doing best at school?"* and *"What are you getting better at?"* The children can draw a picture of their response, and dictate their thoughts to the teacher. The illustration and dictation can be attached to the child's report card or made available at the parent/guardian interview. The child's self-evaluation can often provide a comfortable lead-in to the interview discussion.

The aim of all evaluation is self-evaluation.

The Camel Dances

The Camel had her heart set on becoming a ballet dancer.

"To make every movement a thing of grace and beauty," said the Camel, "that is my one and only desire."

Again and again she practised her pirouettes, her relevés, and her arabesques. She repeated the five basic operations a hundred times each day. She worked for long months under the hot desert sun. Her feet were blistered, and her body ached with fatigue, but not once did she think of stopping.

At last the Camel said, "Now I am a dancer." She announced a recital and danced before a group of camel friends and critics. When her dance was over, she made a deep bow.

There were no applause.

"I must tell you frankly," said a member of the audience, "as a critic and a spokesperson for this group, that you are lumpy and humpy. You are baggy and bumpy. You are, like the rest us, simply a camel. You are not and never will be a ballet dancer!"

Chuckling and laughing, the audience moved away across the sand.

"How very wrong they are!" said the Camel. "I have worked hard. There can be no doubt that I am a splendid dancer. I will dance and dance just for myself."

That is what she did. It gave her many years of pleasure.

Volunteers

Today volunteers are used extensively in many schools and jurisdictions. And many of these volunteers are actively engaged assisting in the kindergarten. With the many learning experiences, and the many demands on kindergarten teachers—including preparing and replenishing materials, listening to individual children as they talk about their work, taking personal dictations, providing direction to individuals or groups to take them to the next step in their work, helping the children to undress and dress, especially in inclement weather—another adult in the environment can be a real lifesaver and can allow the program to expand in response to the many strengths, needs, interests and talents of the children.

Because volunteers, in addition to assisting with the program components, can serve as wonderful kindergarten advocates in the community, I believe that we need to feel secure with our program before we invite volunteers in to help us. Therefore, I would recommend that the volunteer program begin towards the end of the first month of school each year when the routines are in place, the learning environment is well organized, program directions are set, and the children are comfortable in the school environment. Also by waiting until this time, we have more of a chance to determine what roles we want the volunteers to assume—roles that are often determined by the nature of the particular group and individuals within the group.

❖ Getting Parents[*] Involved as Volunteers

In some schools the use of volunteers is school-wide and decisions about whether or not parents will volunteer in the classrooms of their children, if and when parents, or other volunteers, should have access to the staff room, and the particular roles they will serve will have to be agreed upon by the staff as a whole in order to avoid varied expectations. My personal feeling is that if parents wish to volunteer in their children's classes, their requests should be accommodated. There are, however, parents who prefer not to work in their children's classes, and this preference ought to be respected also. I also believe that there are definite advantages for both the teaching staff and the parents when the parents join the staff at the recess times. And in the kindergarten, where a recess break is not part of the teacher's schedule, the volunteer(s) should be encouraged to join the rest of the staff for tea or coffee.

Perhaps the best way to encourage parents to participate in the volunteer program is in a face-to-face situation. Therefore, in many schools the request is made to all parents by the school principal when all the parents are together in the school auditorium at the opening of Curriculum/Meet The Teacher Night early in the school year, or by the teachers back in the classrooms. A letter outlining the volunteer program and including a tear-off sec-

---

*   For ease of reading in this section, the word "parent" is used to refer to parents, guardians or other primary caregivers.

tion on which parents can indicate their preferences—for example, times they are available, grade level preferences, the particular kind of involvements they would prefer in class, their availability for excursions, etc.—can be available on that occasion. For those parents not able to attend the school evening, a copy of the letter can be sent home with the children the following day.

In some schools, kindergarten teachers hold "intake meetings" with individual children and their parents before school begins. These meetings provide ideal opportunities for you to talk to parents about the school's volunteer program. Be sure to give a copy of a letter outlining the volunteer program, including a tear-off section, to the parents to take away with them.

❖ Involving the Wider Community

Many schools, especially kindergartens, also try to involve senior citizens from the local community as helpers. We sent a letter with a detachable reply form to a senior citizens' residence in our area asking for volunteers, outlining the kindergarten program, and indicating that we would arrange for someone to pick up any volunteers and to take them back to the residence at the end of the school day. We were lucky enough to have three volunteers who joined us regularly each week in the kindergarten.

❖ Once You Have the Names, Then Who Will You Invite to Participate?

If the school or particular teachers have decided to make use of volunteers, then I believe that everyone who has indicated a desire to participate should be accommodated. We found in our situation that we had too many prospective volunteers. As a solution, we decided to invite each of the volunteers to participate over a two-month period. In addition to solving the numbers problem and realizing our wish to include all those who had indicated an interest in participating, we also found that this arrangement helped to ease the volunteers into a new role and to sample what was for many, a new experience. Some found that the amount of time they had volunteered was too much; others came to realize that volunteering in the kindergarten was not as they had envisioned and, in a few cases, they requested that they be rescinded from the program before their two-month block was over! Volunteering in the kindergarten is not appropriate for everyone and a two-month period gives the volunteer an opportunity to find out what is involved. You might also review your "contract" with the individual volunteers at appropriate times, for example, New Year, after the March school break, etc.

❖ Preparing the Volunteers for Their Work With the Children

It is important that the volunteers be prepared for their participation in the program. We found that an after-school meeting of all the parents and senior citizens who were going to be involved provided this opportunity. If the volunteer program is to be school-wide, the principal can give an overview of the organization of the program and of the school's expectations of the volunteers; the principal's presentation can be followed by smaller information meetings in the classrooms of the teachers with those volunteers who will be working directly with them. Volunteers should be given an opportunity to ask questions at some point during this meeting.

❖ Working With the Volunteers in the Classroom

I found it important to be well prepared for the volunteers who worked with me in the kindergarten, and determining what I wanted their role to be and what my role was to be was something I had to decide before I met with them at our get-together meeting. It was my responsibility to plan and frame the learning experiences for the children and to provide direction to the volunteers as to their role in helping me to help the children as they engaged in the various activities. As well, I asked the parents and senior citizens to join with me in preparing the vegetables for the snacks, and in preparing the learning materials, for example, filling the paint jars, putting out the varieties of paper needed at the writing centre, sharpening pencils, and filling the glue pots.

During the afternoon, as the volunteers became more familiar with the kindergarten routines and with the location of the materials and the ongoing demands and requests of the children, I found I was more able to focus my own attention on the learning needs of the children and less on the material needs of the program. This freed me to engage for longer periods of time with individuals and small groups. However, I was always aware of my ultimate responsibility for the children and the program and was careful not to make the volunteers feel that they were to feel responsible beyond a certain and reasonable expectation.

Because I had so many who volunteered to participate, I organized the parents and senior citizens into pairs according to their requests for specific days, with each pair volunteering one half day a week. On their first day, I asked the two volunteers to spend their time learning about the program and getting to know the children. Following the children's dismissal, I sat down with the volunteers and we talked about what they had observed. It was at this time that I was able to respond to their specific questions as well as to provide some specific direction, for example: how to take dictation from a child; what to do if a child wants to read to you or to share the contents of his or her language box with you, and the child comes up against an unknown word or a word that he/she does not recognize; what to say when you are responding to a child's work; when is a situation the volunteer's responsibility and when is it mine.

I found that this observation day followed by the talking time gave the volunteers a better understanding of the program and the roles they would assume. The note that I prepared for each on subsequent days (see page 31) gave them the specific direction they needed to carry out their responsibilities on that particular day.

I remember being a little anxious about inviting volunteers to participate in the program for the first time. My uneasiness stemmed from a worry that the volunteers would evaluate and that they might not approve of the openness of the program or the way I worked with or talked to the children. However, because I was aware of the benefits for the children and for me, I knew that it was important to put my fears aside and to reach out and seize what I saw as a wonderful opportunity.

Because we waited until we had the routines in place and until the children were settled into their kindergarten environments before we invited the volunteers to participate, I had time to adjust to the kindergarten and to the children, and to think about how the volunteers could support me. In addition, the meeting we had with the volunteers gave me a chance to describe the program and to realize that many of the volunteers were feeling somewhat uneasy themselves about what was, for some, a new adventure.

By the time the volunteers began to work with me in the kindergarten, I had been able to think through the roles they would assume and to meet each of them personally, and I felt well prepared for their involvement. The opportunity to preplan with Sandra and Joan and to meet with all the volunteers helped me to feel more confident about what I was taking on. Being concerned about what the volunteers were thinking as I worked with the children was something I never got over completely, but maybe that's a very natural, human response. What I do know is that the more I became used to having other adults close by, the more I realized how much they contributed to the program and how much more we were able to offer the children. I'm very glad I took what was for me, a real risk.

The value of the parents who volunteered to our school and, in particular, to our kindergarten were many:

- the parents and teachers came to know one another as people as well as by role;
- a closer relationship between the home and school and between the community and the school resulted;
- parents came to better understand the philosophy of the school and the specific programs in which the children were involved;
- parents working in the same classroom as their children were able to observe, first hand, their children's responses to and participation in the program and in so doing came to understand better their children's learning styles;
- parents who lived in the same community came to know one another better;
- the feeling of a home and school partnership developed.

For the senior citizen volunteers, the experience gave them an opportunity to make a significant contribution and to know that they had knowledge and skills that were valued. In turn, their delight with the children's responses to them was obvious!

Ultimately, it was the children who benefitted most. Having another adult in the kindergarten freed me to do what I had been trained to do—to teach. And that meant I had increased opportunities not only to interact and work directly with the children, but also to observe them as they engaged in their various enterprises. For the children it meant there was another adult to whom they could go for help in solving problems, for direction, for emotional support when needed, and for a quiet, uninterrupted, one-on-one story time.

"Conditions for Learning" in the Child-centred Kindergarten

Learning opportunities and experiences in the kindergarten should be designed to provide a range of experiences to accommodate the abilities and interests of each child. Although large- and small-group experiences form a part of the child's day, it is the more personal and independent self-selected opportunities that are really the heart of the child-centred kindergarten program. Therefore, it is important to build in blocks of sustained time when the children can pursue their natural interests, and explore new learning opportunities that hold personal appeal. The time during which the children choose their own learning opportunities is the time when we get to know the child best because it is most often a one-to-one or, at most, a small-group situation.

Beginning teachers, and those with experience, will find it helpful to keep Brian Cambourne's *Conditions for Learning* (1988) in mind when planning the kindergarten program: **immersion, demonstration, engagement, expectation, responsibility, approximation, use,** and **response.** Cambourne applies these terms first to oral language learning and then to literacy learning. I believe they can also have a more general application when we think about teaching and learning in the kindergarten.

IMMERSION: As we plan the kindergarten program, we need to consider ways of organizing the learning environment and the learning experiences and opportunities to permit the children to *immerse* themselves in their learning. This condition requires block timetabling—the setting aside of periods of extended time for activities rather than short, fragmented time frames—and the provision of ample materials to allow the children the opportunity to sustain their immersion in the learning experience.

DEMONSTRATION: As well as providing children with blocks of time during which they may immerse themselves in their self-initiated, self-directed learnings, it is also necessary that we provide children with *demonstrations* to illustrate how something works, how a story goes, how to find information, how to think through a problem, how to behave in various situations—and the list goes on. Demonstrations are a very important component of the teaching-learning process in the kindergarten to help children gain increased understandings about their world.

ENGAGEMENT: This, for me, is one of the most important, if not THE most important, word when thinking about how we can best provide for the learning needs of children. If one is not *engaged* in the learning experience, then little learning results. And the engagement can be a physical engagement, a mental engagement or both. For a child to be engaged in learning, to me, means that the youngster finds the nature of the learning so compelling, so interesting, so magnetic that the motivation initially to become involved and then to sustain that involvement over time, comes from within rather than from external (and often contrived) motivations. This need for the child to be engaged in the learning is why it is so important for us to get to know the children well—almost inside out—so that we can program from, through, and out of their interests, strengths, and talents.

EXPECTATION: It is important that children have *expectations* for the particular learning experience in which they are involved. A learning experience can hold a kind of promise for the child based on pleasurable past experiences, and the knowledge and insights the youngster brings to the situation. The more experiences the child has had with the learning materials or the topic under discussion, the clearer the expectations will be for that youngster. That is why it is so important that children have frequent opportunities to work with familiar materials and to talk about things they know about and care about. Not only will their expectations be clearer, but they will be able to enter the experience with greater self-confidence and assurance that they will be able to succeed.

As well, it is important to the learner that the teacher have expectations too. Kindergarten teachers need to set objectives, and in these days of "Outcomes-based Education," expectations become very important. When the children are working with new material the teacher's expectation is that the children will experiment with the material to learn about what it can and cannot do. As the children's familiarity with the material increases, expectations change and, in fact, become more diversified as different children work with the material. For example, when Peter was working with math materials, I had certain expectations for him and these were different to those I had when another child who was not so mathematically aware as Peter was working with the same material. Setting objectives with the child helps the child to determine a direction and to work towards desired outcomes. This is not to suggest that before a child uses the material or equipment that the product is to be determined, but rather that whenever possible, the child should be given the opportunity to voice what he or she is doing and the teacher—following the child's lead—should make suggestions or add an additional challenge.

RESPONSIBILITY: In a kindergarten in which the children make many of their own choices and decisions within the context of their school day, much of the *responsibility* not only for learning but also for personal behaviour is given to the children, with the teacher taking more of a back seat in terms of the role he/she plays. It's not easy for us as teachers to give this responsibility over to the children—especially in the early years of teaching. However, if children are to be self-motivated and self-directed learners, it is necessary that we give the ownership for learning and a greater share of the responsibility for their own actions to the children. To do so requires that we have a working knowledge of the developmental characteristics of young children, the way kindergarten goes, the expectations of the school community, and an understanding and appreciation for our own abilities and talents. Transferring the classroom focus from ourselves as teachers to the children as learners is a process that may take considerable time. However, I see it as vitally important that we do so.

APPROXIMATION: This is an interesting term to consider when looking at learning across the day. It has such applicability not only to the children as learners but also for us as evaluators of the children's progress and accomplishments. As the children grow and learn, experiment and discover, we can see through their repeated exposure to learning situations and their handling of materials and equipment, that their *"approximations"* become more "exact" over time. For example, we might observe a kindergarten child who is having a first-time experience using paints. The child will have, perhaps, a sense of how to hold the brush, how to dip it into the paint and how to transfer and apply the colour to the paper. However, for the first few tries, the result may include paint in unexpected places, and a not-so-successful application of the paint to paper. Eventually, with repeated practice, the child will become more adept at using the medium and at producing results that are more personally pleasing. It is both expected and desirable that the child go through the process of experimentation and discovery—of approximation—as a way of learning.

USE: In a child-centred kindergarten, children are *users* of time, space, materials, and human resources. Through practice, they learn to use time, space, and materials more productively, and to make use of their peers, their teacher and the adult volunteers as supports to their learning.

RESPONSE: Today's kindergartens are filled with the sounds and the busyness of children *responding*—responding to stories, to songs, to discussions, to their emotions, to investigations and to discoveries. In fact, children need to be actively engaged in responding to all the ongoing learning experiences in which they are involved. It is therefore important that we remember to build in lots of time for such response because it is through response that the child comes to understand what he/she knows and feels. Again, this active encouraging of response is part of the process of giving the responsibility for learning to the child and it may take time to feel comfortable doing that.

Group Dynamics

Kindergarten children are energetic, curious, and egocentric. In combination, these qualities make each child very interesting; however, when multiplied twenty-fold or more times over, the result is a group of youngsters whose collective energies and curiosities are boundless.

When working with the whole group it is necessary to keep the learning experience—reading to the children, singing with them, taking group dictation, etc.—moving along at a pace that will sustain the children's interest. Finding that pace was not easy for me. It took some weeks for me to find the pulse of the group and to be able to ask the right questions, to make the right eye contact at the right time, to engage particular individuals in some form of active participation, or to slow the pace or speed it up when necessary.

Small group work presented me with a different challenge—that of entering into an experience in response to the group's starting point. For example, when moving into a group-selected activity, I first had to look at what was going on and to listen to what was being said among the group's membership. To do so required patience on my part to resist the temptation to jump right in!

For groups that were working well, my entrance into their activity usually took the form of questions, for example: "*What are you doing?*" "*Who's doing what?*" "*What's next?*"

For groups that weren't working productively and that needed help in getting along together, my intervention was usually more focused and direct, for example: "*What's the problem?*" (I think it's important that the children themselves identify the nature of the difficulty: it's their problem, not ours; they must be able to agree on the difficulty they're having so that any assistance we might be able to provide will, in fact, be in response to the real problem and not in response to the perception we have. The talk that occurs at this stage can also sometimes solve the problem or suggest a solution or a course of action that we can take.) Once the problem was identified by the group, I would ask how they thought the problem could or should be solved. Often the solution they suggested was that a certain group member shouldn't be allowed to play with the group! On rare occasions, this *was* the appropriate solution and I would ask the child to choose another place to work or to take time out by sitting quietly until ready to rejoin the group. More frequently, however, I found that such a solution was, at best, only short term. And so, I preferred to allow the child to continue to work with the group and to tell the child that his or her behaviour wasn't acceptable and to give the child some direction, for example: "*Let the other children have a turn too.*"

I came to realize that many of the difficulties within the groups arose because kindergarten children find it difficult to determine the roles that need to be played out, and then to identify who will do what. A little role definition was often all that was needed, for example: "*John—you could work on the turret*"; "*Mary—why don't you make the boat?*"; "*Robert—someone needs to build the drawbridge; could you do that?*"

Once I had learned that young children who chose the same activity or chose to work together sometimes found themselves in difficulty because they were unable to define roles for themselves within the activity, I would often ask the group of children to remain behind for a moment and we would talk about their plans for working together before they actually went to their workplace. On other occasions as soon as all the children were at their workplaces, I would go directly to those areas in the kindergarten where groups of children were going to be working together, for example, the house centre or the blocks, to make certain that the group was getting off to a good start.

Usually it was one of the children who would come to me to tell me that the group was having a problem. I saw this request for help as a healthy first step because it meant that the children were identifying the fact that there was a problem—that something was getting in the way of productivity. Of course, everyone in the group had his or her own version of what the problem was, and although it was sometimes difficult, I tried to be patient and to hear the children out first before offering suggestions or direction.

Resolving group conflicts with children of this age is not easy because it's difficult for the young child to reason through the situation. Therefore, when attempting to provide a solution to the problem, I would ask the children, *"Is that a fair way to solve the problem?"* because I think it's important for children of all ages to know that a fair solution is important. And it's also important not to make any child feel that he or she is to blame, but rather to deal with the situation as a problem that requires a solution. The more quickly the difficulty can be resolved the more quickly it can be forgotten and the children can get back to their work.

Establishing a group dynamic with four- and five-year-olds is difficult; sustaining it is even harder!

Learning Centres

The children are the curriculum—the program content comes from them, from what each does at the learning centres.

Learning centres operate on the premises that not all children can learn about everything there is to learn, that not all children need to learn the same things, and that not all children learn in the same ways. Very sound premises, to be sure! So much has been written about young children's learning centre-based programming that it would be redundant to discuss all the whys and hows of such programming at this point. However, if a variety of centres is available for use by children, a variety of learning is made possible. Indeed, the more centres we can provide, the broader the base we have upon and through which we can build our program.

We must decide, in advance of setting up our learning centres, **what** it is we wish the children to learn—not so much in terms of content, but rather: attitudes, appreciations, self-discipline, decision making, cooperation. The fact that a child creates a specific product is not the first and foremost concern. The children's attitudes towards learning, their abilities and their willingness to listen and to respond to direction, to cooperate, to share

materials, to assist and to receive assistance from others—these are the very important learnings.

An appropriate balance between process and product is the key. Finding that balance is the challenge!

Some teachers suggest that activities should be introduced slowly; others believe that the children should be given a variety of activities from which to choose right from the start. I think this choice is a matter of personal taste. Some teachers' strengths lie in the ability to organize well and to model their organizational skills with the children by introducing a few learning centres with well-defined routines. Other teachers' strengths lie in being able to keep on top of many activities, and to develop rules as needed. For the latter group, the attention is less focused on pre-organization and more towards dealing with and solving problems as they arise.

However we choose to implement our learning centres, it is important that we organize the program so that the time spent at the centres becomes for **all** children the **major** focus of the kindergarten program.

The number of centres is, of course, dependent on the physical space available. The centres should include activities designed for both individual and small group work. Activities should vary in nature. Manipulation is important; sensory experiences are vital. Some centres will be creative (for example, art, construction); some may require more exact direction (for example, games such as Snakes and Ladders); while others will be of a more aesthetic nature (for example, collections, some craft activities).

Many learning centres will be self-directing, and the children will know what to do with the material or equipment because the material or equipment is self-explanatory or may be used in any ways that the children view as possibilities. Blocks, cut and paste, crayons, painting, and dress-up are just a few of the self-directing centres one would expect to find in the kindergarten.

Materials should change throughout the year. In September, large manipulative materials and equipment might catch the child's interest. For some, it will still be the large equipment that intrigues in June. And, of course, sand, water, and blocks have a place throughout the year.

Number games and "reading" games (matching, sorting, sequencing) will appeal to some throughout the year.

Creative junk, painting, colouring, paper, scissors and glue have seasonal appeal—every season!

But what about the child who chooses the same activity(ies) every day? Kindergarten and primary teachers are still discussing this one. There must be a special magic about the activity that we don't see that keeps calling the child back. I think it's important to spend time observing the child at the activity to try to determine what the attraction is. Often we will find that the attraction is that the child feels comfortable and successful at that particular centre. And I do believe that each time the child revisits a centre that he or she learns something new because inherent in each activity are extended learning possibilities. For example, if the child chooses blockbuilding regularly, the child can learn the names of and how to differentiate between and among geometric shapes, about weight (which feels heavier to you, the cube or the cone?), about length (which block is longer/shorter?), about size (which is bigger/smaller?). The child can learn what is possible to build and what is impossible, which blocks rest comfortably on others and which do not, which are best for a foundation....And with encouraging and appropriate questions we can lead the child to new learnings and further understandings.

Some of the learning centres that might be found in a kindergarten are

The Permanent Work Areas
- painting
- listening station(s)
- sand
- water
- blocks—large and small
- cutting and gluing
- house centre—dramatic play
- puppets
- colouring
- writing centre
- reading centre
- games
- math centre—with a variety of manipulative materials
- climbing and sliding
- building/construction
- dress-up

The Changing Work Areas
- wood gluing
- box sculpture
- straw blowing
- sponge painting
- seasonal centres (displays, art and crafts relating to the season)
- colour centres—continually changing throughout the year
- toys and games that change according to developmental levels
- interest centre—store, hospital, gas station, etc.
- collections—rocks, favourite books, trophies, toy cars, etc.

Permanent centres provide security for the children; the changing centres reflect children's changing interests and needs, and provide additional challenge and surprise. They also serve to extend the child's imagination and to heighten interest.

❖ Getting the Learning Centres Underway

After we decide on the number of centres we think we can handle comfortably, keeping in mind the number of children there will be in the group and the size of the kindergarten room, we will need some beginning materials and equipment. Assume, for example, that your beginning centres are going to include the following: classroom library/reading corner, creative art, drama and puppets, mathematics, painting, sand, science, social studies, water, writing, house centre, building/constructing, grocery store. Then you might gather the following materials:

- **classroom library/reading corner**—book racks (free standing if possible), rocking chair(s), books, magazines, taped stories and tape recorder, class-made books, filmstrip projector, etc.
- **creative art**—crayons, coloured pencils, scissors, felt pens, an assortment of paper, popsicle sticks, straws, cone cups, Plasticine, glue, string, tape, and so on. As children always find a creative use for anything, this centre can accommodate just about any materials you can find.
- **drama and puppets**—a few commercially produced puppets, a puppet theatre if possible (although you can always improvise with a desk turned on its side or with a large cardboard box). To this centre, the children can bring the puppets they have created at the art centre. Materials, fabrics and castaway teacher clothes for dress-up can look great on young people!
- **math centre**—anything you can find for counting, measuring, building—blocks, interlocking cubes, abacus, scales, measuring tapes, geoboards, games, feltboard, cooking utensils, geoblocks, buttons, dice, calendars, egg cartons, bottle caps, hundreds board, math storybooks, etc.
- **painting**—easel (or two), floor space for those who prefer not to paint at an easel, laundry flakes, plastic paint containers, brushes, paint, and paper to start. There are so many other materials to which you can introduce the children when you involve them in special painting techniques. Eventually this centre will require a lot of space in the classroom, and it should become very popular!
- **sand**—sand table, sand, scoops, shovels, moulds, sieves, spoons, dust pan, brush, pails, hand lens, watering can, models, little cars, etc.
- **science**—hand lenses, thermometers, equal-arm balance, metre sticks, magnets, terrarium, batteries, hand mirrors, giant magnifier stool, measuring tapes, flashlight, basic microscope, etc. Some of these items might have to go on your "Wish List" for a future time!
- **social studies**—globe(s), wall map (displayed low so the children can see it and touch it—the floor is a wonderful surface for a map if you can afford the space!), magazines, local road maps, old telephone books, files of interesting pictures that are community-related, simple puzzles, and certainly many pairs of strong legs for the many walks in the community that you will take with the children throughout the year to observe and experience the various seasonal and community changes!

- **water**—water table, water pumps, non-toxic bubble soap, vinyl eye droppers, buckets, squirt bottles, clear vinyl hoses, flexible tubing, plastic pails, funnels, strainers, measuring cups, sponges, things that float and things that sink.
- **writing**—a variety of writing surfaces, for example, paper, empty scrapbooks, magic slates, chalkboard space, little chalkboard slates, envelopes, acetate sheets, etc.; a variety of writing tools, for example, magic markers, pencils of varying sizes and thicknesses, crayons, chalk, etc. Again, this is a centre that will grow and grow throughout the year as the children take greater interest in communicating their ideas through writing. Some of the children may want to begin their own writer's folders in which they can collect their writing.
- **house centre**—table and chairs, plates and cutlery, refrigerator, stove, sink, shelves, ironing board, broom, tool set, "groceries," telephone, writing tools and pads for grocery lists and telephone messages, dolls, highchair, stroller, dress-up clothes
- **building/construction**—hollow and solid blocks, building bricks, Lego, straws, cardboard boxes of various sizes and shapes, interlocking bricks, various commercially made construction toys
- **grocery store**—and more!—tables and shelves (for display), adding machine or calculator, toy cash register, empty foodstuff boxes, empty tin cans and containers with labels on and lids off, empty tin cans and containers with lids off and with no labels so children can make their own labels, papers and pencils, magic slates, aprons, Post-its to affix prices to items, Bristol board cards and markers for labelling purposes, and an array of art materials (for example, crêpe paper) with which the children can design uniforms to identify specific jobs, and building blocks and boxes so children can build the store

Through the year, the grocery store can change into a hospital, a gas station, a toy store, an airport, a restaurant, a clothing store, etc. With some paints or crayons for a new sign, and the art materials for the uniforms, the conversion can be fast.

Air Canada, Flight 625, is now ready for take-off at Gate 2!

As the children convert the grocery store to a hospital, make a quick visit to the school library to locate and borrow "hospital books" for the book centre. These books can be used by the hospital "architects" for reference both in the designing and equipping phases of the construction.

Many children will want to make labels to post around the centre—airplane, mother, baby, doctor, nurse, flight attendant, ticket taker, gas tank, garage, emergency room, etc.

Some of the children will want to print the names on strips of
Bristol board, staple, and wear them as headbands
to identify the specific roles they are playing.

*"That comes to four dollars and fifty cents. Here's your change.
Have a nice day!"*

If you can afford the space, having more than one of these "flexible" centres available all year round for the children is worthwhile because they can acquire so much language and learn so many life skills through their involvement and interactions. When we returned from our trip to McDonald's a small group of children immediately got some building blocks and boxes, and made their own McDonald's in the kindergarten and played out the roles they saw various McDonald's personnel assuming.

As learning centres are set up, it's a good idea to keep a running record of other centres that could be introduced in the future, and to keep an inventory of what will be needed to make each centre operational. The following chart may be useful in planning for those future inclusions:

Possible Future Learning Centres' Checklist
LEARNING CENTRE:
SPEND MONEY ON:
MAKE OR COLLECT:
IDEAS FOR ITS USE: (where? when? how?)
AUDIO VISUAL AND SPECIAL EQUIPMENT:

Getting Organized for the School Year

As beginning teachers, or as teachers about to begin teaching in a new school, you should ask yourself: *"Where should I focus my attention to help ensure that the children and I get off to a good start in the kindergarten?"* There is so much to think about when starting out on a new venture, and at times you will feel overwhelmed! This is natural, and to be expected. The suggested list of "helps" that follows is by no means complete; however, I hope that the suggestions will be of some assistance and, perhaps, will generate some further ideas.

❖ Prior to September

- become familiar with the school community—take a walk or drive around the area and try to soak up some of the atmosphere
    - does the school have a lunch and after school program?
    - if so, do many children go to the after school program?
    - do the children live in apartments, houses?
    - do the children play outside after school?
    - are there parks nearby where the children can go to play?
    - where is the nearest public library?
    - what facilities, in general, are available to the children and their families?
- make an appointment to visit the school where you will be teaching so that you can meet the principal and staff
- if possible, meet the current kindergarten teacher(s) and visit the kindergartens during school hours to become acquainted with the programs, and the equipment and materials available
- request copies of any curriculum guides (for more about curriculum guides see pages 128-9) that you will be expected to use, and any others that might be of use to you
- ask for a tour of the school in order to get a feel for its size and a sense of its routine and rhythm
- visit your Board's professional library and the public library, and borrow some articles and books relating to kindergarten that you think might be of help for teaching kindergarten and for giving you an understanding of the nature of the age group with whom you will be working

❖ As You Begin to Plan for September

- think about the room arrangement—which centres and where?
- think about a beginning timetable and how the day might go (see "Learning Centres," pages 4 and 105-11, and "The Planning Board," pages 114-17)
- gather up materials from around your home for which you no longer have use (see pages 9-10), but that could be used by the children at the house centre, the building centre, the craft centre, etc.

❖ As September Approaches

- gather up books to read to the children, and music books with fun songs to sing with the children
- spend time in your kindergarten—arranging furniture and, once arranged, stocking the centres with materials that the children will need to work there (it's always a good idea to talk with experienced teachers about materials—they will have many suggestions for you)
- put up some appealing pictures and posters, etc., for the children to look at, and put out some interesting collections for the children to look at and handle, for example, buttons, stones, little cars. Do remember that what you display should be purposeful and should serve to catch and capture the children's interest and imagination. Don't put up so much that you fall into the interior decorating trap! You will want and need lots of space for the children's work!
- spend time thinking through your first day—overplan rather than underplan, but be ready to postpone some of your ideas for another day (things just don't happen as quickly in reality as they do in our minds!!)
- as you work through your first-day plans, keep thinking *"What will the children be doing at this point and what will I be doing?"* Try to envision how a learning experience might proceed—make mind pictures with both you and the children in them!

❖ The First Day and Beyond

- keep "balance" (see pages 131-2), "responsive teaching" (see page 30), "direct instruction" (see page 48), "whole group, small group, and personal learning experiences" (see pages 103-5) in your mind as you plan for each day
- provide learning opportunities that will let you get to know the children, for example, outdoor play, learning centre time, games with name cards, Show and Tell
- begin to work out a method for monitoring and tracking what you need to monitor and track, but be careful not to overdo it. We can become so preoccupied with tracking and recording that there's little time left to do anything else! (For more about "Assessment and Evaluation," see pages 85-95.)
- don't feel rushed, and try not to rush the children
- enjoy the children and above all, remember—"The expert in anything was once a beginner."—this statement applies to adults too!—no one expects you to learn everything there is to know about teaching overnight!
- do the best you can, and continue to read...and to grow...and to learn!

The Planning Board

When you plan your learning experiences for the children you should try to do so so that the learning experiences for each day will grow naturally out of one another and so that each day will flow more smoothly into the next. With all of my teaching—whether it be four- and five-year-olds or adults at the university level—I am guided by the words *function* and *form*. For me these are the two most important words to remember as we set out to plan any learning experience.

Function **precedes** *form.*

It is so important that we know **why** before we determine **how**. In other words, we need to think about our purposes/objectives for the learning experience, and then determine how best to frame the experience to achieve the desired outcomes. With this approach in mind, as a major component of my planning, I made use of a public **Planning Board** that the children checked each day as soon as they came into the kindergarten.

This Planning Board was a large chart paper account of how the day might unfold, in the order of how things might go. At the beginning of the year I used my own very unartistic sketches to indicate the various experiences. Over time, I introduced words and phrases to support the sketches. In this way each child could choose to read either the sketch or the print, or both. Later in the year I replaced the individual words and phrases with sentences; however, the sketches remained to ensure that all children would be able to read the chart. For those children who could read the sentences, the sketches served as a confirmation of their understanding of what they had read.

I began each Planning Board chart with a welcome to the children before launching into the content of the day. Following the welcome, there was often an instruction for the children to follow, for example, *"Find something yellow."* We would then look at what the children had found and talk about some of the objects. On other days the Board might say, *"What day is it today? Tell a friend."* Or maybe the children would read, *"Count from 1 to 10." "Count backwards from 10 to 1."* This kind of instruction would set the room humming with the sound of numbers. It was fun to hear the children trying to see how far they could get and we would laugh together when they got in trouble and just couldn't remember what number comes after 8 when you count backwards!

On other days the children would read, *"Please go to your work now. We will have a story soon."* Quite often our program started this way, especially in the winter months when snowsuits, boots, mitts, and scarfs took up much of my time and I didn't want those who were ready to get going to have to wait.

I tried to bring a variety of introductory activities to The Planning Board, not only to ensure that the children would not have to experience the

From...

The Planning Board near the beginning of the year

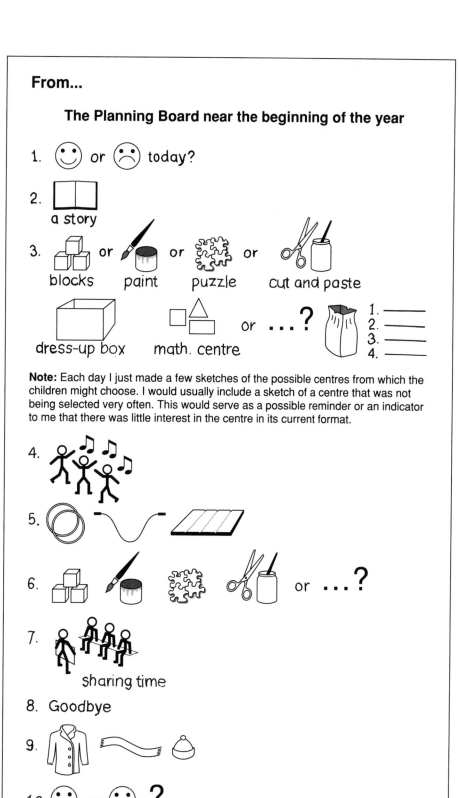

1. :) or :(today?

2. a story

3. blocks or paint or puzzle or cut and paste

   dress-up box   math. centre   or ...?

Note: Each day I just made a few sketches of the possible centres from which the children might choose. I would usually include a sketch of a centre that was not being selected very often. This would serve as a possible reminder or an indicator to me that there was little interest in the centre in its current format.

4.

5.

6. or ...?

7. sharing time

8. Goodbye

9.

10. :) or :(?

same routine day after day, but also to engage the children in a variety of cross-curricular learning experiences that are an important part of the ongoing program, for example, reading nonfiction to them, playing math games together, engaging cooperatively in an experiment with magnets.

To...

The Planning Board – later in the year

Good afternoon boys and girls. I am so happy to see you here today.
Please jump up and down 10 times and then sit down.

1. I have a good story to read to you today.

2. It's time to go to our work. Do you know where you want to start today? Who brought a Show-and-Tell bag?

    John   Martha   Kesin

    _____ _____ _____

    Who would like to work at The Special Table with Mrs. Jones?

    Dick   Timothy   Carolyn

    Samara   Romana   _____

3. Let's sing and dance.

4. Today is gym day. Let's have fun.

5. Go to your work and then we'll tidy up.

6. Let's share now.

7. Let's sing "Goodbye".

8. It's time to get our coats and hats – it's cold!

9. I hope you had a happy day at school. I'll see you tomorrow. or ?

The Planning Board was a wonderful opportunity for so many learning experiences. Not only did we have the chance to read for authentic purposes, but also we could talk about what we would be doing 4th, 2nd, etc. We could tell what we would be doing before...and after....The Board provided the children with an ever-available reference to what was coming next and it also helped to keep me on track. As well the Board served as an effective and comprehensive daily planning record.

Often before the children went home we would talk about things the children wanted to do the next day, or maybe a story they'd like to hear, or hear again, or a special art activity they would like set up. I would often try to build their suggestions into the program either for the next day or the day after.

As soon as the children had left the school grounds and were safely on their way home, I would sit down with my black magic marker and the chart paper, and would record the menu for the next day, keeping in mind the suggestions made by the children.

I found The Planning Board to be a most important and successful technique both for programming and for reflecting purposes. By the end of the year I had 184 charts that served as a reminder of the various and sundry activities in which the children and I had engaged. As well the charts provided me with an opportunity to see how much the children had grown in their ability to engage in more challenging activities, to take risks, to read, to compute mathematically, to make decisions and choices, to follow directions—and so much more.

Singing With the Children and Engaging Them in Musical Activities

Every child deserves music provided regularly in a well-balanced program. Not all children will be vocal stars—I certainly found this out very quickly!! However, this is not to suggest that children shouldn't sing. Precision in vocal undertakings should not be of prime importance. In the kindergarten and well into the primary grades, children are still finding their singing voices. Many children do not, at four or five years of age, sing in key. Musical activities that focus the child's attention on listening carefully will help to develop the ability to reproduce vocal sounds more accurately. Songs that are short and simple can be learned easily and, through frequent repetition, can be of assistance in helping children become more accurate in their reproduction of vocal sounds.

Rhythms should be a daily component of the music program. Echo clapping and variations seem to be enjoyed by most children. The active components of rhythmic activities catch the interest of young children, and such activities encourage and develop cooperation, critical listening, and sensitive observation by the children. Orff and homemade instruments can be used effectively in the kindergarten music times.

Listening to music can be relaxing for children. Young children deserve to hear classical music as well as children's songs and contemporary music. Melodic selections from the classics can provide an introduction to a form of music not often heard by many children.

Singing provides a wonderful, low-risk opportunity for students in today's increasingly multi-ethnic, multi-cultural kindergartens to practise using English. Singing songs that bring alive the cultural backgrounds of the children will both acknowledge the diversity of cultures represented by the children and delight the children as they sing songs that originated in their country of birth or that of their parents.

❖ What We Did, Why We Did It and How We Did It

For me, music times were important times of every day. We would gather together at The Meeting Place (see page 43 for more about The Meeting Place) and participate in a variety of musical and music-related experiences. Usually we began with some kind of rhythmic activity—often echo clapping. I would clap a simple beat to get us started and the children would repeat the beat as a group. As their success with this activity grew, I would incorporate some rhythms that they would then echo. Often I would ask a child to invent a rhythm and we would listen and then repeat it. (This required very careful attention on my part to make certain I was hearing what I thought the child was trying to do!) In addition, we would often get our feet to stomp out the beat or rhythm and when the children were ready, we would combine the two. Instead of hand clapping, the children liked to try finger snapping. Most found this difficult, but they wanted to keep trying. We laughed a lot during finger-snapping time because so many of us had so much trouble. It was fun!

And, of course, we sang. We learned a new rote song just about every day, and we would sing the song day after day until we felt pleased with our performance.

We also spent a lot of time marching, galloping, and skipping in time to the piano music. We listened to the high notes and we stretched our bodies up, and then as the notes got lower and lower, we began our descent to the ground and curled up in little tiny balls on the floor. We listened to Beethoven and Chopin and we danced around the kindergarten space in personal response. We tried to tone-match (I'd sing or hum a note and the children, or a child, would sing or hum the note back) with some of us having more success than others.

To get around the problem of my singing voice being an octave below those of the children, I often invited individual children to sing the note and we'd all try to sing it back. We talked about and listened to sounds to determine which were higher, which were lower, which were louder, which were softer. I printed the lyrics to songs we had learned on chart paper so we could "read" them as we sang along.

We also had great fun singing and acting out the action songs we were learning. "The Hokey Pokey" was a favourite as the children tried to figure out which was their right hand, and once they had that under control, then wherever was their right foot? We sang songs about animals as we prepared for our trip to the zoo so that at any time one looked into the kindergarten, one might see a herd of elephants lumbering around the room singing at the top of their lungs!

During music time I always included

- the singing of favourite songs we had learned
- a new song that integrated what we were talking about in the kindergarten or reading about in our read-to time
- a participatory time when the children would be free to move about the room in response to music
- a time for the children to listen and respond to clapped beats and rhythms, or piano music played loudly, softly, in a low or high register, at a fast or slow speed

For me, music time was one of the best times to observe the children. I learned a lot about their ability

- to listen
- to discriminate
- to identify likenesses and differences
- to memorize and recall
- to respond accurately to beat and rhythm

And because so many of these skills are closely aligned to the skills of reading, I found looking for correlations very interesting. Were, in fact, the children who were able to distinguish differences in sounds, to memorize song lyrics with relative ease, to echo clap accurately, the same children who were moving more quickly into reading? Although there were a couple of exceptions, I found that generally there was a positive correlation, perhaps because both require a sense of rhythm (the rhythm of music; the rhythm of language), and careful attention, listening, and recall.

Our music times together each day throughout the year became very special and important times for all of us. I remember them very fondly!

Just a Suggestion: For those who may feel a little uncomfortable singing *to* the children, try singing *with* them. Most children know a number of songs, and several songs will be known by many of the children. Ask those who know the song to start singing it and then you join in. There are also a variety of taped songs for children available (by Sharon, Lois & Bram, Fred Penner, Raffi) that you can enjoy with the children. Many of the youngsters will learn the songs quickly and as soon as they begin to sing along with the tape, you can join in too. Once you feel comfortable, try singing the song with the children without the tape. You'll be pleasantly surprised at how well you do!

"A Little Whole-class Math Won't Hurt"...I Told Myself

Just as I read regularly to the whole class, sometimes I engaged the whole group in a mathematical learning experience. Sometimes the learning was little more than a rote counting experience; other times we would try to guess, *"What number comes after...?"*, or, *"What number comes before...?"* The children enjoyed talking about and learning about shapes, so sometimes we found ourselves looking at triangles and squares and such, and talking about how they were different and how they were the same. Using non-standard units of measure we would try to guess how many steps we would have to take to get from one end of the room to the other, or how many seconds it would take us to walk (not run!) to the gym for our physical education time. We kept a monthly chart of the height and weight of each child and, with sensitivity when necessary, we talked about who had put on weight, who had grown taller, and who had stayed just the same. When we got a new game in the classroom we would often come together to have a quick play to see what the game was about. The children loved to roll dice, and to play tic-tac-toe using the commercial playing board and plastic x's and o's. Checkers was another favourite and we enjoyed playing cooperatively, with each of us taking a turn moving a checker on the board.

This group time was not designed to teach mathematics to the children in a formal way and there were no pre-determined specific learning outcomes. Rather, it was a time to think about mathematics, and to learn and use the language of mathematics during a short, highly active and interactive time together. It also provided me with a fast and wonderful way of collecting ongoing information about the children's attitudes, knowledge, and developing skills and awareness—information I could store away for later use.

Just a Suggestion: At your Meeting Place keep a box of math materials that you can use to introduce new ideas and concepts and to revisit the familiar. A deck of playing cards, cards with hand-printed numbers, a few geometric shapes, a pair of large dice, sorting and counting materials, a metric stick, measuring tape, and a trundle wheel can provide you with opportunities to explore a variety of math experiences as you gather together or as you wait for a few children to join the group, as a quick break, or as a link from one experience to the next.

Show and Tell—Also Known as "Show and Lie," "Drag and Brag!"

Initially this was not one of my favourite times to be sure! I found it difficult to observe the children's disinterest, and yet I believed that Show and Tell provided a wonderful opportunity for children to talk to their peers about things that interested them. And I know it's important to give children, from an early age, opportunities to share with others what they know about and care about. However, there was just too much disinterest on the part of too many children to sustain Show and Tell in the format I had established, with all the children sitting together while one child stood up and told his/her story followed by the next and the next and the....And so, one day I asked those children who were going to be bringing something for Show and Tell the next day to bring it in a bag, to keep what they'd brought a secret, and to put the bag on the counter until it was time to share their treasures.

The idea turned out to be a great success. We had to try to guess what was in each bag, and soon the children caught on to the idea of asking questions as a way of narrowing the possibilities. Each day I invited the children to decide how many questions—between five and ten—could be asked. A child would print the numeral on chart paper to remind us and then as each child shared his/her treasure, another child would keep a tally of the number of questions asked. Some children learned to tally like this IIII III, while others preferred to record the numeral that corresponded to the number of the questions asked. After a time, however, I noticed that the interest of some of the children who had not brought something to share was waning again. And so, I took the process one step further. We had our Show and Tell time when the children were working at the centres, and only those children who had brought something to share needed to come to the group. Of course, everyone was welcome and, in fact, many others did join us—often because they liked to ask questions and to try to guess.

Eventually, as the number of learning opportunities in the kindergarten increased and time became even more precious, Show and Tell became a Mondays-only happening. The children had become more interested in sharing and talking about their ongoing classroom projects, and bringing something from home didn't seem to have the same appeal that it once had.

Show and Tell provides a wonderful opportunity for children of differing cultures to bring in objects representative of their cultures and to talk about them, and to answer the many questions that the other children will have. It can be a wonderful time for us to learn so much about the practices, beliefs, and customs of various cultures and religions. And most of the "teaching" can be done by the children while we, along with the other children, engage in the question-asking portion of the discussion. The children's "need to belong" (Maslow—see pages 133-7) can be strengthened by such an experience. In addition, it may be possible to have some of the parents come into the classroom (with the principal's support) to talk a bit about their homeland and to share some of the customs and artifacts of their native homes. As well, for English-as-a-Second-Language children Show and Tell provides a wonderful opportunity to hear language that focuses on a specific object or relates to a specific experience.

For the teacher, Show and Tell provides myriad opportunities to introduce and develop new vocabulary, to build information, and to encourage a greater understanding, respect, and appreciation of the various cultures represented by the children.

Show and Tell was the very best part of school for me, both as a student and as a teacher. Not recess or lunch, but that special time set aside each week for students to bring something important of their own to class to share and talk about.

As a kid, I put more into getting ready for my turn to present than I put into the rest of my homework. Show and Tell was real in a way that much of what I learned in school was not. It was education that came out of my life experience. And there weren't a lot of rules about Show and Tell—you could do your thing without getting red-pencilled or gonged to your seat.

As a teacher, I was always surprised by what I learned from these amateur hours. A kid I was sure I knew well would reach down into the paper bag he carried and fish out some odd-shaped treasure and attach meaning to it beyond my most extravagant expectation. It was me the teacher who was being taught at such moments.

Again and again I learned that what I thought was only true for me...only valued by me...only cared about by me...was common property.

Show and Tell was a bit disorderly and unpredictable. What the presentations lacked in conventional structure was compensated for by passion for the subject at hand.

Just a Suggestion: However you decide to program for Show and Tell, consider making participation a *choice* for the children rather than making the activity a *mandatory* one. Obviously the children who have brought something to share will participate; however, for the others the decision as to whether or not they will participate as audience could be left to each child to decide. Of course, an invitation to participate should always be extended to all children.

Learning With Nursery Rhymes

Nursery rhymes can serve as a springboard to the many learning experiences with poetry that you and the children will share throughout the year. Some children may have had little if any exposure to nursery rhymes, while for others the poems will be so familiar that they will delight in chanting along with you. Through several repetitions, I encouraged all the children to commit many of the selections I read to them to memory, and I encouraged the children to chime in as the selections became more familiar to them.

I often recorded the children's favourite rhymes on experience chart paper and displayed them at eye level around the classroom. A picture or sketch on each rhyme chart simplified recognition considerably! These charts became invaluable as breakthroughs to reading for a number of the children.

Many children wanted to paint a picture of their own "crooked man who walked a crooked mile," cut and paste their own version of the "Three Blind Mice," cook and decorate their own "Humpty Dumpty" and, working with some classmates, construct a large "Humpty Dumpty" wall, or a crayon "Little Bo Peep" as she's rounding up her lost treasures. And what fun it was to dramatize—

"Who wants to be Bo Peep?"
"Do I have ten volunteers for sheep?"

Just a Suggestion: The book *Once Upon a Golden Apple* by Jean Little et al contains illustrations and text relating to many of the children's favourite nursery rhymes and fairy tales; they provide "golden" opportunities for children to chime in and to enact roles. You could chart the responses in order:

"NO";
"NO, NO, NO";
"NO, NO, NO, NO, NO!"
"YES!"

and the children will delight in being able to join in on their cue! And who can resist reading and dramatizing *The Jolly Postman* by Janet and Allan Ahlberg?

Working Together in the Gym

Climbing, swinging, jumping, and rolling provide endless opportunities for developing skill and control of personal response. Purposeful and imaginative action results from floor activities and apparatus work.

—*Education in the Primary and Junior Divisions.*
Ontario Ministry of Education.

Come together in the kindergarten, put on running shoes, and move to the gym; spread the equipment about the space; as few rules as possible but be sure to remind the children what the safety rules are; the child makes a choice from the variety of equipment available; catching, skipping, scoring a goal, balancing, trying a front roll, climbing, running, hopping—stop in the middle—*"everyone sit on something green"; "hop on your right foot to something yellow"; play "What Time Is It Mr. Wolf?"* and then carry on...

*Time in the gym and outdoors for a young child—for any child—*is vital for healthy growth. The gym class should be an active and challenging time for

children during which they have the opportunity to develop skills in handling equipment, body awareness and coordination, rhythm and grace in movement.

I made certain that we got to the gym as often as possible. We used as many of the recess periods as we could when the rest of the school children were outside. We only had fifteen minutes on those occasions but that was certainly enough time for the children to run off some of their energy!

I found that the more open the program in the gym, the more beneficial and productive it was for the children. By "open" I do not mean there were no limits or parameters, but rather that within the established parameters—that is, where particular equipment was to be used, the safe and appropriate use of the equipment, and the expectation that we would play well together—the children were given a lot of freedom to choose their equipment and to decide how they would use it.

I also found that the skills of physical education often developed from free play. For example, children who have had experience using balls of various sizes and weights will eventually be able to use them in a wide variety of structured situations.

We began our year in the gym with lots of equipment—for example, large and small balls, benches, hula hoops, bean bags, ropes, etc.—and a great variety of usage. The children found something familiar, something comfortable. When they had finished with a piece of equipment they were free to put it back and make a new selection. As the year progressed, the children used the same equipment but at a higher level of skill. As well, I noticed that the children began to invent group games using the equipment and to play in a more cooperative and collaborative fashion.

We went outdoors whenever the weather permitted. The outdoors provided opportunities for swinging, sliding, running, and jumping in an aesthetically pleasing environment. On those days we moved some of the gym equipment outdoors for use in the fresh air and sunshine.

I found there was such a range in the children's developmental levels that it wasn't reasonable to expect common achievements or accomplishments by all the children in the gym. And so I organized the space with a variety of equipment from which the children selected. Throughout the gym time I instructed the children individually and/or in small groups as appropriate. At the end of the session, before the equipment was put away, I would ask certain children I had observed, or with whom I'd worked, to bring a certain piece of equipment to the centre of the gym and, with the others seated around, demonstrate for us what they had learned.

Just a Couple of Suggestions: Be sure to find out what the safety requirements are for the use of the various kinds of equipment in your gym. Obtain and study information from both your school and your Board.

Check with your Board to see what gym equipment it might have that your school does not have that can be made available to your school on occasion.

Whenever weather permits, take the children outdoors to play. Young children love to run and to run off steam, and they don't need a lot of equipment to engage in healthy activity. Even something as simple as a walk can be an invigorating experience for the children. As often as possible, include outdoor activity or a visit to the gym as a daily component of the kindergarten day.

Part IV:
Frequently Asked Questions About Kindergarten and Programming for Young Learners

Teaching young children is not easy! This section—in which I ask and respond to some of the questions that are often asked by parents, by administrators, or by other teachers, as well as questions we ask ourselves—is included to assist those of you who now teach or who are looking towards a career teaching young children.

It is impossible to identify all the questions that one might be asked and, of course, some of the answers will vary depending on the particular community, and/or the educational jurisdiction in which one teaches.

I hope, however, that some of the questions that follow are ones you've been asked, will be asked or maybe have asked yourself, and that the answers provided will be helpful as you continue your very important work with young children.

1. What are the objectives of the kindergarten program?
I see the program objectives as being very broad-based because the learning outcomes will vary from child to child. The program should provide opportunities for every child to develop physically, intellectually, socially, personally, and spiritually. But the growth for each child in the areas identified will be uneven. For some there will be tremendous growth in small and large muscle development and control; for others the growth spurt may be in the area of social development. And other children may grow in leaps and bounds intellectually. Therefore, we must not expect the same learning profiles to emerge for all children. Rather, we must plan programs and provide learning opportunities that support and encourage children in their involvements across the learning spectrum. This means that an appropriate range of learning opportunities must be available to the children across the learning day so they may participate actively in opportunities that promote physical, intellectual, social, personal, and spiritual growth.

In short, I believe our primary objective in the kindergarten is to nurture the children as self-directed, self-motivated problem solvers, and to respond to their individual abilities, strengths, and talents. If we can do that, we will have provided a wonderful service to the young learners.

Most of what I really need to know about how to live and what to do and how to be I learned in kindergarten.
  Wisdom was not at the top of the graduate school mountain, but there in the sandpile...
    These are the things I learned:
      Share everything.
      Play fair.
      Don't hit people.
      Put things back where you found them.
      Clean up your own mess.
      Don't take things that aren't yours.
      Say you're sorry when you hurt someone.
      Wash your hands before you eat.
      Flush.
      Warm cookies and cold milk are good for you.
      Live a balanced life—learn some and think some and draw and paint and sing and
          dance and play and work every day some.
      Take a nap every afternoon.
      When you go out into the world, watch out for traffic, hold hands and stick together.
      Be aware of wonder...
      And then remember the Dick-and-Jane books and the first word you learned
          —the biggest word of all—"LOOK."

Just a suggestion: Posted in every kindergarten, Fulghum's kindergarten learnings can serve as an ongoing reminder to all kindergarten teachers of what is really important for children to learn during the kindergarten year(s). And posting the list on the wall outside the kindergarten can be a reminder to parents and visitors, of the importance of the kindergarten year(s), too!

2. How did you make use of your local kindergarten curriculum guides to help you plan for a learning centre-based program?

I find that curriculum guides are **very** helpful to me as I set about the task of organizing a teaching program, no matter what grade I am going to teach. And so, I went early to the guides that my Board of Education had available for kindergarten. But I used the guides more to get **a sense of what teaching and learning in the kindergarten were about,** rather than as **a recipe for *what* to teach and *how* to teach it.** Of course, I paid attention to the content suggested, but I tried to look at that content as a **direction** for programming rather than as the program itself. There are also certain expectations that parents have, that administrators have, and that I have for the kindergarten years, and I found that the curriculum guides put me in touch with those expectations.

Once I had more or less internalized the content, the directions and expectations, then my job became more of an imaginative one—figuring out how to program to incorporate the content and expectations through a program that reflected the way children learn and through an atmosphere that promoted self-initiation, self-direction, decision making, etc. At all times, I tried to think of interesting ways of providing the content through the learning centres and materials I was planning for the kindergarten rather than using the content to plan lessons to be "taught" to *all* the children. I wanted the kindergarten to be **our** kindergarten, not **my** kindergarten, and it took me a while before it began to feel that way!

3. How does one plan a timetable to accommodate the variety of interests, capabilities, learning styles, backgrounds, and background experiences of so many children?

When I was preparing myself to teach kindergarten, this was a question that haunted me. How would I ever meet the learning needs of all the children at all times? Well I think the honest answer is that I don't believe we can. I know I didn't, although I tried very hard to do so. I was, however, guided by a very strong belief system about how children learn and I found *Maslow's Hierarchy of Needs* particularly relevant and helpful:

- children's need for physical well-being
- children's need to love and be loved
- children's need to belong
- children's need to achieve competence
- children's need to know
- children's need for beauty and order

Using this list of needs as a guide, I could plan my timetable and organize our day with a greater sense of purpose and direction (see also pages 132-7). For example, the list strongly suggested to me the need for variety and balance in the program. There needed to be

- time for teacher-directed activity, and lots of time for child-directed activity
- time for working alone and times for working together
- time for the children to work with me—individually, in small groups and in whole-class arrangements (with the emphasis on the first two)

I also recognized the need for children to work at self-initiated tasks and, at times, to engage in learning experiences that were more of a teacher-initiated and teacher-directed nature.

I found that as I became more comfortable, I could become increasingly more responsive to the directions in which the children took me. For that reason my timetable changed frequently throughout the year.

I did, however, always include times for coming together as a group—to sing, to be read to, to talk about things that were of general interest to us, to make plans, to share. I also always planned for extended blocks of time when the children could choose from and work at the variety of activities that were available in the learning centres in the kindergarten.

Show and Tell was eventually reserved for one day a week (see Show and Tell, pages 120-2), and except for a period of about one month when the children all came together for a snack, snacks were simply made available to the children, and they could build a nutrition time into their day whenever they wished. And so, although the timetable was rarely static for any prolonged period of time, it often followed a pattern similar to the following:

- children arrive and come together
  ...a story, a song, a cooperative game, a listening experience, a talk with the children about how the day might go
  ...introduce new activities, remember unfinished work from yesterday, special times
- children make the decision about which learning centres they will work at first...and away they go!

and

- come together as a group for song and rhythms
- snack time
- as a group visit the gym on Wednesdays and Fridays
- as a group visit the library on Thursdays
- welcome the Grade 6 children with whom we are paired off for a reading to/listening experience on Tuesdays (see "The Buddy Program," pages 83-4)
- Show and Tell when appropriate
- clean up...not a favourite time for the children or for me! (see pages 63-4)
- children come together...a story, a song, a cooperative game, a listening experience
- goodbye...the song...the hugs...scarf tying...coat zippers and buttons...boot buckling...and out!

or a variation:

- entry and gathering together for hello's, attendance, and a look at the plans for the day (see pages 114-17)
- making decisions about which learning centres we want to begin our work at for the day[*] and off to those centres

---

[*] At these times I would often read to the children. I considered the read-to time an important time of the day and an important program component (see page 80). And so I read to the children as often as we could find the time. They loved to listen to stories and poems and I loved to read them, so these were always great times for us!

- time out for singing as a group, galloping, and all those other things that little children love to do in response to music (see pages 117-19)
- back-to-work at the learning centres
- clean-up time
- sharing time
- story time

4. Today we hear so much about "balanced programming." What were your considerations in trying to achieve balance in your program?
For me, **balance** was probably one of the most important considerations in my attempt to design an appropriate program for the young learners. I considered balance from the following perspectives:

- balance between teacher-directed and child-initiated learning experiences
- balance between large and small group, and personal learning experiences
- balance between directed/planned teaching and responsive teaching
- balance between process and product
- balance between progress and achievements/accomplishments
- balance between my input and the children's output, between teacher direction and the child's initiation and self-direction
- balance between cognitive and affective learning experiences
- balance between expressive (child talk) and receptive (teacher talk) language experiences
- balance between "soft" and "loud"—the quieter and the noisier times
- balance between indoor and outdoor activities (weather permitting)
- balance between and among the listening, speaking, being read to, and viewing/observing learning opportunities
- balance between my time with the children and their time with their work (a time in which I would play the companion role)
- balance between...and...

Trying to determine the appropriate balance in each was difficult. Rarely was it a 50/50 proposition. For example, the balance between teacher-directed and child-initiated activity was probably more 30/70 on most days; between process and product 70/30; and expressive and receptive language experiences 65/35. These ratios would vary depending on the particular day and sometimes on the mood and the energy level of the children. On some days, the children would have been content to sit and listen to story after story if I had let them. That never happened, but I must admit that on such days I would read more often, or for longer periods of time than usual. On most days, however, the children were filled with energy, and just getting them to come together for a brief period of time was, for me, a major accomplishment!! I began to look at balance more in terms of balance over the week rather than over the day. Taking this approach seemed to allow me to be more responsive to the directions of the children.

5. Kindergarten programs are often unit- or theme-centred. How did you incorporate these into the program?

I must admit that I have reservations about centring the kindergarten program around units or themes. I personally find them too confining, too restricting, and in certain circumstances, too contrived and contriving. What I'm referring to is a program in which *all* the centres, *all* the songs, *all* the stories, and so forth, relate to a particular unit or theme. A theme-centred program certainly helps teachers to organize, but I don't believe that children think in themes or pre-packaged units. Moreover, although most units or themes will have appeal for some children, not all children will have the same commitment, and it becomes difficult to hold their natural interest and curiosity over a sustained period of time.

Certainly in our kindergarten we always had a topic focus, for example, our colour of the month, the seasons, and our class trips for which we prepared and followed up. Although we generally focused our attention on the topic for brief periods of time only, the topics did help to unify our sense of community, and to give us something in common to talk about and think about. During our group times we found it valuable to have a focus for our discussion as these talks often led some of the children into further explorations of the topic through picture-making, looking at books, modelling, sand-building, etc.

Quite often our Special Table would have an activity available related to our topic/focus. However, I believe such topic-focused inclusions at the learning centres and special tables should be *in addition* to the choices and opportunities already available. By incorporating the topic into the existing centres through the *adding* of ideas and materials, we can extend the range of possibilities for the children's thinking and doing, and can augment the number of learning opportunities to which the children can bring their imaginations and their ingenuity.

6. How did you go about creating the learning environment once you had your furniture and supplies?

For me, this was a difficult task. I must add, however, that I found room arranging difficult when I taught first grade, eighth grade, sixth grade....I have yet to plan or to see the perfect room arrangement and I have yet to hear a teacher say that he or she has found it.

Much of what I did was very much trial and error, and I found myself rearranging the furniture often, to suit the changing needs, interests, and experiences of the children. For example, when some children began to take a more independent interest in being with books, I enlarged the book corner. That meant that another area had to be decreased in size or eliminated for a period of time. Sometimes, certain work areas were not being used as frequently or by as many children as I would have expected, for example, the cut-and-paste and house centres. In such cases, I initially thought that I would simply remove the centre. However, because I believed that the learning opportunities at that centre were not only valuable ones but also something that I thought would have interested the children, I decided first to move the centre to a more visible and accessible area in the classroom, and to hold a little meeting with the children to talk about the centre's new location, and to review with them some of the possibilities for its use. The results were usually very impressive! Often the demand for the centre far exceeded the space available, so we increased the space. On other occasions, however, all my attempts to convince made no difference whatsoever; the centre remained empty and so I packed it up and replaced it with something new.

Again I was guided by certain beliefs about how children learn, and I found this knowledge helpful in designing a classroom for four- and five-year-olds. There needed to be a space for being together, and there needed to be lots of room in which children could move about freely. Art centres need a sink nearby, just as a filmstrip machine and computer need wall sockets. As well as floor space, building blocks need a storage area; the sand and water tables work better in a tiled floor area so that the many spills that are a natural part of the learning process for young children can be accommodated. I tried to minimize the number of tables in the kindergarten so that more floor space would be available, as I found that for many of their activities the children were as happy working on the floor as at a table. Manipulative materials went on shelves, on tabletops, or in the case of the blocks, in the storage cart; pencils and magic markers found their home in empty juice cans, and every child had both a cubbyhole and a bin for personal storage. Although the physical arrangement of the classroom changed frequently, I found the organization illustrated on the next page worked well for the children and me.

Maslow's Hierarchy of Needs came in very handy, not only when I was setting up the kindergarten initially, but even more so as I rearranged it throughout the year.

Children's need for physical well-being

I found that it was important to provide comfortable places for the children to work and to recognize that what I deemed comfortable was not always what the children saw as comfortable!! And so, I provided lots of floor space where the children could work—for their building projects as well as for writing, looking at books, and playing with board games. Tables and chairs were provided for those who wished them, although I was careful not to have too much furniture of this type because of the amount of space it required. Cushions and pillows were also available to the children for their comfort.

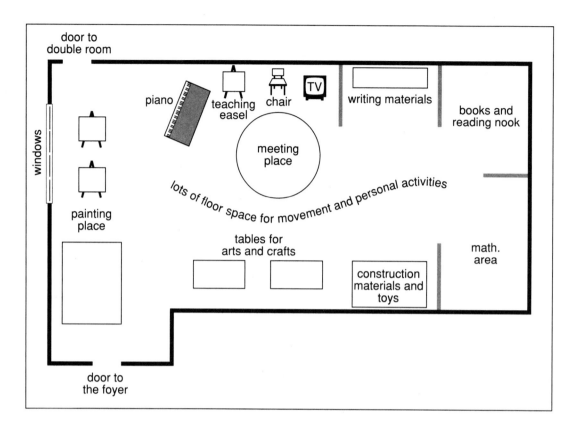

Children's need to love and be loved

This need is important to all human beings—not just to children. However, it is especially important for young children. And so, from the first day, I made it my responsibility to ensure that I knew each child's name, and I did whatever I could to make sure that all the children knew that I cared about them. Some of the ways in which I tried to do this included responding favourably to their work (see pages 137-8), calling them by name, encouraging them to talk to me, and showing genuine interest in what each child was saying. Basically what I was trying to do was to build up a caring atmosphere in the kindergarten where the children felt secure, comfortable, cared for, and cared about.

Children's need to belong

This need is also very strong in all adults, and so important in young children. It was one of the reasons I was so insistent throughout the year that, in addition to providing time for the children to work independently, in pairs, and, on occasion in small groups, we engage regularly in whole-class learning experiences so that we could come to know one another better and so that I could ensure that the talents and abilities of **all** the children were recognized and appreciated. I worked very hard during these times to develop a strong sense of community among all of us—and it did take a while for this community spirit to develop!

Children's need to achieve competence

Some of the children came into the kindergarten on the first day with their competence very much intact! These children quickly emerged as natural leaders, and the most frequent contributors to every discussion—no matter what the topic! It was important to me to sustain their spirited attitude; however, it was important—in fact, vital—that I also focus on those youngsters who didn't seem to have the same degree of self-assurance. For me, the best way to ensure a feeling of competence in these children was to acknowledge regularly and often the many accomplishments they were experiencing in as many areas as possible. *"Good for you!" "You do that so well!"* and *"What a great start!"* were frequently heard. I also encouraged the children to compliment one another on their progress and achievements. I have to admit that providing this regular and ongoing support took a great deal of concerted effort on my part to keep it front and centre in my mind and to make certain that I acknowledged equally the progress and achievements of **all** the children—not just those whose capabilities were so obvious.

Children's need to know

Young children have an insatiable need to know! In the kindergarten, one question seems to piggyback on another. *"What's this?" "How does this work?" "Why does...?"* permeated the kindergarten every day. Young children, being the self-motivated learners that they are, truly want to know. In order to satisfy this need I did my best to respond to the stream of questions that faced me continuously each day. I once heard it said, *"The only dumb question is the question that isn't asked"*! And I do believe that, because it is by asking questions that we find out those things we want or need to know about. And so, I constantly encouraged the children to ask questions.

Another way in which I tried to respond to this need to know was to include a little section of program each day in which we would all come to-gether to talk about something and go away with new information. Such sessions included talks about "space," "dinosaurs," "why the sky is blue," "how magnets work," etc. Many of our knowledge-seeking talks focused on the area of science, an area that held great fascination for the children and for me (although I found that in some cases the children had more of the answers than I did!).

I do believe that it is in trying to encourage questions by the children and by deliberately providing thought-provoking, information-seeking learn-ing opportunities that we sustain the child's natural curiosity and, I would hope, encourage the youngsters to find joy in learning so they will, in fact, be lifelong learners.

Children's need for beauty and order

This need I found the most difficult to sort out and respond to because as it is said, *"Beauty is in the eye of the beholder."* And I know from personal life experience that one person's perception of "order" is often not shared by others!

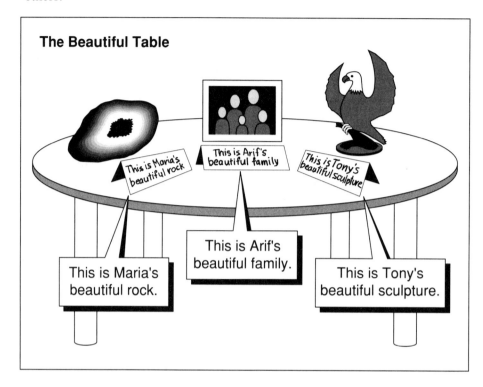

The Beautiful Table

This is Maria's beautiful rock.

This is Arif's beautiful family.

This is Tony's beautiful sculpture.

    I tried to bring beauty to the classroom by filling it with brightness and colour, by displaying children's work in every available space, and by setting up a "Beautiful Table" on which the children could put objects they thought were beautiful. This idea immediately caught the interest of the children and the table was always full. The Beautiful Table provided the youngsters with an opportunity to bring their personal definitions of beautiful to the situation, and to stand back and feel a sense of pride in their contributions to the collection.

    I dealt with the issue of order in a very different way in that I let the children show me what their senses and degrees of need for order were. Some of the children found order by working in a mess of papers and implements. It seemed their order was pre-determined and they gathered everything they might need for their project around them at one time. Others would, or could, only deal with immediate needs, and so I would find those children with only paper and scissors and, when they had finished with the scissors, they would put them back where they belonged. And then they would get the crayons. It was quite a contrast! But all styles—including those that fell somewhere between the extremes—had to be equally appreciated. My role then became one of sorting out the child's personal style and responding to it by suggesting where the child might wish to work (to ensure ample working space), and by providing ongoing support—and sometimes direction—to help the child to be able to sustain the task through to completion. Although the children went about their tasks in very different ways, they seemed to get to the same ends upon completion. I must admit that watching how the children approached their various enterprises and how they sustained personal interest and motivation was a source of constant fascination and pleasure for me.

Tidy-up time was another opportunity for me to see what order meant to individual children. Some seemed very content with their contribution if the building blocks ended up somewhere near the storage cart, while others would spend what seemed to me to be an inordinate amount of time making certain that the piles of construction paper were in perfect order—and colour-coordinated!!

Through my ongoing observations to determine what I needed to do to respond favourably to the variety of need for order that existed, I also became aware that the children had to become responsive to the kind of order I needed to keep the kindergarten running relatively smoothly. For example, I would explain to the children that because there were so many of them and only one of me, that it would really help us all if they remembered to put things back where they belonged when they had finished with them, that when I had something important to tell everyone they should stop what they were doing so we wouldn't have to spend time waiting for a few to be ready to listen, and that they should come and tell me if we ran out of certain materials because I might not have noticed. And so, for certain, we were all sharing the classroom responsibilities together.

7. We all want children to be successful in their learning and to enjoy their learning involvements. Was there any one thing in particular that you found made a real difference to the way the children approached their work and how they felt about it?

Well there are many things we do in the kindergarten that enhance learning and encourage success, from singing favourite songs to listening to favourite stories. However, there was one thing in particular that I found made a real difference. And that was the language I used to respond to and to encourage the children as they went about their work. It's so important that we speak to children in ways that will keep them moving forward, and I think that **what** we say to children as we work with and alongside them is crucial in helping them to develop the kinds of positive attitudes that we want so much for them to have as lifelong learners. It wasn't easy for me—there were moments and even days when I didn't feel very positive about myself! And sometimes while driving home from school I would reflect on something I'd said to a child during the day and find myself wondering why I'd responded in such a way. I began to realize how **very** important supportive language is and how negative criticism really doesn't help the young learner—or any learner of any age. And so, I began to listen to myself a little more closely, and in some cases to be a little less impulsive when responding.

What follows is a beginning list—it's still a "work-in-progress"—of what I hear teachers saying to children in classrooms where the attitude of the youngsters is positive towards their learning, and where the children seem to value their accomplishments and themselves:

- good for you!
- how are you doing?
- any problems?
- any questions?
- have you thought about...?
- what have you decided about...?
- what will you need to...?
- what are you doing?
- tell me about...
- we seem to be having a problem with...any ideas about how we might solve the problem?
- where will you be working now?
- what did you learn today?
- who can help_____ with _____?
- if you need my help, let me know.
- yes!
- yes you may!
- yes you can!
- who would like to ...?
- thank you!
- terrific!
- fantastic!
- way to go!
- I'm proud of you!
- isn't it wonderful that...!
- you have made a terrific start at ...

I'm certain that there are many more words and phrases that can, and will be added to the list. The important thing is for us to remember that our language can either be inviting or disinviting; encouraging or discouraging; interesting or disinteresting; forward- or backward-leading....I think it's important that we stop and listen to the messages we are giving the children by what we say to them.

8. Once the children had arrived and were settled into the kindergarten classroom and the kindergarten "routine," what did you find took up much of your time in keeping the program going?
For me, the housekeeping items seemed to be the most time consuming. Filling the white glue jars, mixing paints, replenishing paper, etc., were necessary jobs to be sure, but I found these tasks took too much of my time. And so, very soon after the school year had started, I enlisted the help of older children in the school and, later in the first term, the volunteers who

came in to help each day. The children helped me for twenty minutes before our kindergarten class started, and because their classes began fifteen minutes after the kindergarten, they were able to stay with us and help the children to get a good start on the day. The adult volunteers were a wonderful addition to the program. Not only did they assist with the housekeeping kinds of tasks that were so necessary, but they also helped the children with their work at the centres, listened to a child read, read to a child or a small group, or just sat and talked with a child and gave that child the most precious gift of all—the gift of time!

We had many days when neither the older children nor the adult volunteers were available and we managed just fine. It took a little longer for me to get to the paints to replenish them or to get the vegetables ready, but the children came to understand and accept the delays. I came to very much admire and respect their patience because I knew it wasn't easy for four- and five-year-old children to have to wait to finish their paintings or to fill their hungry stomachs!

9. What was the expectation for you in terms of your communication with the home regarding the progress of the children?

It was expected by my Board of Education that we would establish regular and ongoing communication with the home. Mandatory communication included three report cards a year—one at the end of each term; an interview with every parent/guardian towards the end of the first term (early December) and a second interview with as many as possible towards the end of the second term (mid-March).

I found that my communication far exceeded the mandatory expectations. As in many kindergarten situations, some parents appeared at the kindergarten door at both entry and dismissal times. So, for these parents two interviews a day became the norm! Most parents, however, could expect several telephone calls during the year from me and a minimum of two invitations for an interview at report-card times.

We gave the children's families an overview of the kindergarten program at our Meet the Teacher night at the end of September. At that time I asked that if any parents/guardians needed or wanted to talk with me about their child they get in touch with me and I told them that I would do the same. Some took me at my word and would drop me a note requesting a telephone call or an interview. If there was a real problem of some kind, I would call and set up an interview or talk it out over the telephone. Most of my telephone calls, however, were to share good news or to ask questions about something I had observed. For those children who were from single-parent/guardian families or homes in which both parents/guardians worked during the day, I would write a short note asking the parent/guardian to give me a call at the school whenever it was convenient for them. And I would tell the children what the note was about so they could verbally pass the message along. Only in an emergency would I disturb a parent/guardian at work, for example, if the child became ill, to check on a child's absence, if the child arrived at school upset about something, etc.

I found interviews to be particularly good times for expanding on and embellishing my report-card comments, and for describing in the case of those whose children were experiencing some form of difficulty at school, the kinds of steps that the parents/guardians and I might be able to take together to help the child, and to improve the situation.

There were, unfortunately, a few parents/guardians who were not able to keep in as close touch as I would have wished, so I just did my best to reach them through brief notes and the work the child took home to put on the refrigerator!

For those whose children were experiencing some difficulties at school and with whom I was not able to make or sustain direct contact, I found it necessary to be a little more direct in terms of what I wrote on the report card to ensure that the parents/guardians were aware of the difficulties the child was having. Although I was always honest in these cases, I tried to be very careful to communicate the difficulties in forward-looking and helpful ways.

Like my Board, I believed in good communication between the home and the school, and I think we should try, as best we can, to establish a comfortable rapport with the child's home. For that reason, before the children went home each day, the children and I would talk a little about some of the things the children had done that day that they could report on to help keep the home in touch with the school and the program.

Just a Suggestion: If you are having the parents/guardians in for a Meet the Teacher/Curriculum Night at which you are going to talk with the families as a group about the kindergarten program: be certain to have adult-sized chairs available and arranged where the parents will be able to see and hear easily; use overheads to guide your talk and to help keep you on track; use children's work when possible to illustrate a point; consider posting signs above the various centres that outline the learning possibilities, for example, "Why Sand?..." or "At the block centre, children learn...". Make certain you cover what you want parents to know about the program, and then open the discussion to respond to questions the parents may have.

10. What was the most frequently asked question by the parents/guardians, and how did you respond to it?

The question is easy to recall: *"How is my child doing and will he/she be ready for first grade?"* The answer to the first part was relatively simple because I could describe for the parent what the child was doing in the kindergarten and my observations of his/her progress. The second part of the answer did not come so easily for me because never once did I think it was my job to prepare any of the children for Grade 1; rather I believed my job was to work with the "now child"—to support and encourage the children through the challenges of the day. Many of the parents, however, obviously thought it was indeed my job to prepare the children for the first grade! What I didn't want was to get into was a description of my educational philosophy at that time. Fortunately, because I had previously taught Grade 1 I knew the kinds of things that go on in Grade 1 classrooms, and so I would identify the kinds of abilities, skills, and attitudes towards learning that the child was acquiring through the kindergarten experience that would serve him or her well in the program the following year. I talked more of such things as concentration, memory, perseverance, and decision making, rather than does the child know how to add numbers together? is the child beginning to read?—or as some of the parents would have preferred, "can the child read?"—and would cite situations and observations whenever possible to support my comments.

I always welcomed questions concerning a child's progress at school for two reasons: I enjoyed sharing with the parents/guardians what I knew and was learning about the child, and I appreciated that it was interest in their child's well-being that prompted the question.

11. When parents ask how they can help their children at home, what should I tell them?

In my current role as a program coordinator, this is a question I'm frequently asked at parent/guardian sessions. And I must admit that it's difficult to answer in such a group setting because each child is different, home expectations of and for the child are different, and expectations of the school vary from home to home. However, I do think there are some generic suggestions that we can offer to those parents/guardians who want to support their children in direct ways during the kindergarten year(s).

• *Encourage your child to talk about what he/she is doing at school.*
And I would explain: As parents, when we invite our children to share school experiences, we are indicating to them that we value education, and that we are interested in hearing about how they are spending their days.

• *If possible, provide some materials in the home that are similar to those found in the kindergarten, for example, books, an assortment of writing implements, picture-making implements and materials (crayons, paper), construction toys and materials, games.*
And I would explain: Providing such materials indicates to the child our support for the school program, and gives the child the opportunity to practise and to demonstrate his/her progress and accomplishments.

• *Make time to listen to your child.*
And I would explain: As well as serving as an audience for our child, by giving our youngster the opportunity to talk to us we are also providing the time and attention that every child needs.

• *Invite and encourage questions from your child.*
And I would explain: By asking questions children reveal their sense of wonder and curiosity about their world. As parents, when we invite our children's questions we are supporting and helping to sustain their curious nature.

• *Read to your child daily.*
And I would explain: Bedtime is often the most convenient and the most relaxed time for reading to children at home. Through this experience, not only does the child have the opportunity to listen to selections of his/her choosing, to learn more about books and from books, but also the child gets the parent's/guardian's undivided attention for a sustained period of time.

• *Offer praise liberally!*
And I would explain: Children like to know that they are valued and there is probably no better way for us, as parents, to show them how much we value them than by supporting their efforts to grow, to learn, and to be sensitive, caring people, and by acknowledging their progress and accomplishments— not by external rewards, but rather through the "well done," "good for you," and "thank you" that children deserve to hear often.

• *Enjoy your child!*
And I would explain: Every child is unique, with talents, abilities, strengths, and needs that are different from those of other children. It is important that we value who our child is and enjoy his/her uniqueness.

• *Think and speak well of the school.*
And I would explain: Attitudes we hold as parents are transferred to and felt by our children. Therefore, if we want our children to think well of the school, it is important that we speak of the school in positive terms. This does not mean that we should not acknowledge any concerns we might have—by all means we should. A telephone call to the school, or perhaps an interview with our child's teacher and/or the school principal is most appropriate and will be welcomed by the school personnel.

There are, of course, many other suggestions that we can offer. I have found in my experience that families are appreciative of any help we can give to enable them to encourage and support their children in the beginning years at school.

12. Using the information you had collected throughout the term, how did you go about writing report cards about these young learners?
The purpose of the report card is to permit one human being (the teacher) to report to a second human being (the parent/guardian) about the school progress and achievements of a third human being (the child). Although

writing report cards is a time-consuming undertaking, I have to admit that I rather enjoyed the experience! And this was true no matter what grade I was teaching. I still have not figured out why I enjoyed it, but I did. Oh, there were certainly times through the process when I wished I only had one more to write...and there were still several to go! But all in all, I found writing reports cards a mind-stimulating and challenging experience.

Again I was guided not only by my Board of Education's directions concerning report-card writing, but also by my personal belief system concerning the report card and its purpose. I wanted to report on important matters—**behaviours** that had made a difference in terms of the child's progress at school. I wanted to tell the parents/guardians what their children were doing during their hours at school and with what results. In short, I wanted to tell a story—a whole story about the child, using language that would be meaningful to the parents/guardians and that would leave them with a tremendous sense of pride in their child. It always took me a few drafts of the early writings to be able to write with a measure of success.

The kindergarten report card for which I was responsible was anecdotal in the first term, and a combination anecdotal/checklist format in the second and third terms. I certainly preferred the anecdotal report because it meant that I was in charge of deciding the content, although I was guided by the categories that were listed down the left-hand side of the form.

I began the writing task by working through the report cards in alphabetical order; that system usually broke down by about the third or fourth report when I was faced with the name of a child who needed a little more thought time on my part before I committed my observations to paper. And so I would move on to the next one.

The difficult part for me was always the getting started time. Finding a block of relatively uninterrupted home time was the first challenge. The second was getting myself in the right mood for what lay ahead. And then there was the problem of finding my writing rhythm. That was sometimes the most difficult of all!! However, once I had all those challenges under control, the *real* problem arose—**what** should I write?

Armed with my anecdotal notes about each child, checklists, some work samples, and *a lot of observations of learning situations in which the child had been involved stored in my memory* (see "Assessment and Evaluation," pages 85-95), I set out on the adventure. It was, of course, important to include information about which parents/ guardians *wanted* to know, but it was also important to tell them about things they *needed* to know. The former was often the academic progress of the child, but what I wanted to tell them focused more on the human qualities of the youngster. And so I combined the two information perspectives into the story, and wove both through the fabric of the text I was creating.

Finding the right language to communicate my enthusiasm was not easy. I needed to find just the right phrase or adjective to describe the painting, or to capture the child's surprise and excitement at the moment he/she figured out that those squiggly marks on the page translated into words and those words translated into meaning!! And being truthful at all times required that I find just the right words so that the child's self-esteem would always be protected.

I was also very careful to avoid making predictions—the *"If John does this, then this will happen,"* kinds of statements. As we know, there are no guarantees in life and we can't ever be absolutely certain that what we think will happen will, in fact, happen! So I was careful to stick with what I knew through my observations of the child over time.

I also had to make certain that I commented on growth in all areas of development for which I had responsibility. And I always wanted to do this in a positive, forward-looking, and helpful way, even—and perhaps especially—for those children who were having problems of some kind. It was important to me to write honestly about the child's progress; however, I would often save additional information and embellishment for the interview so that the parents/guardians and I could talk face to face about the problem or difficulty in an attempt to decide how the home and school could work together to help the child.

I felt strongly that it was important to record and describe the children's strengths. I wanted to know what the children's strengths were, and I was certain that the parents/guardians wanted to know too—often as a confirmation of what they already knew about their children.

And I also saw some necessity to record weaknesses or limitations—those things that gave children difficulty, sometimes to such a degree that for various reasons they might never master them but would, instead, have to learn to accommodate—perhaps throughout their lifetimes. I never saw it as my job to criticize a child, but rather to describe the child as honestly as I could and then, when necessary, tell the parent/guardian what I was doing to help the child in a particular area.

But a third category intrigued me the most. This is the area of what I call **becoming strengths**—the behaviours, the abilities, the talents that at a particular time may not be well developed, but that show possibility and promise. That is, with the right kind of experiences, the appropriate instruction and direction, and the proper amount of encouragement and support, the becoming strength could quite well, in time, become a strength. An example would be the child who sings with beautiful tone and diction but has not found the right pitch. Rather than seeing this particular characteristic as a weakness, because the sound and diction are so good I would see great possibility for getting the child to sing in key, and I would use some very direct teaching strategies for helping him or her to do so.

As I began to learn more about the children, I began to focus more and more on their individual strengths and becoming strengths and I put the areas of concern over to one side. I didn't forget about them, but I tried to put the emphasis on what the child **could do**, and what the child was indicating he/she was **moving towards** being able to do.

13. Many jurisdictions are moving towards the possibility of full-day kindergarten programs for young children. What are some of the programming considerations that one would want to think about when embarking on such a new venture?

I think that there is growing agreement that full-day kindergartens are very much on the horizon, and that within a relatively short period of time we may see the possibility change to probability, and then into reality. And I think that it's important that we plan for this reality in positive and forward-looking ways.

There will be the technical obstacles to overcome, of course: space, busing, lunch arrangements, the increased numbers of teachers required, to name just a few. However, with careful pre-planning I think these challenges can be overcome and worked out to the satisfaction of all.

Program considerations become very important and must be considered thoughtfully and thoroughly prior to the implementation of the full-day kindergarten.

I would think that the first agreement in any jurisdiction would have to be that **we wouldn't want the kindergarten to become a first-grade program.** Because the children are spending a full day at school does not mean that they are any more ready for the more formal education that one might find in a first-grade program. The children will still be four- and five-year-olds, and will be bringing their four- and five-year-old characteristics, interests, and talents with them. These characteristics we cannot change—nor would we want to!

As teachers we will have to remember that with double the amount of time we will have with the children, for some of us (the more impulsive type—and I certainly include myself in this group!) it might be difficult to resist the temptation to double the program!

And so, my recommendations would include **maintaining and sustaining the current philosophy for kindergarten program design:**

- play-based
- responsive to the children's interests, experiences, talents, abilities and competencies
- teaching that recognizes and respects the children's physical, intellectual, emotional, and social (PIES) stages of development
- open, flexible programs that respond to and support the children's leads and directions

The most significant change I would make would be to take the most obvious limitation of the half-day program and use it to advantage. And that limitation is **TIME!!** But rather than doubling the duration of a learning experience (for example, reading twice the number of stories or singing twice the number of songs at any one time), I would spread the experience out across the day. In fact, to start, I would be inclined to duplicate the program sequence for both the morning and afternoon. In this way, the children would have two blocks of time to work at the learning centres; two opportunities to come together for songs and stories and talks (not to mention two opportunities to practise putting on snowsuits or to search for lost mittens!!)

Certainly an advantage of the full-day kindergarten is that children can leave their works-in-progress from the morning to the afternoon, and from the afternoon to the next day. This was a benefit that the children in my class had before we joined with the other two kindergartens in December. Until that time no one used our kindergarten room during the morning and so we were able to leave our unfinished paintings and our completed block structures overnight. We missed being able to do this when we were no longer able to leave our work for others to see, or to leave something not finished until we returned the next afternoon.

When thinking about a full-day kindergarten program, a consideration of the following would be beneficial:

- the implications of a full-day kindergarten program for a young child
- ensuring that the current kindergarten philosophy is maintained
- making use of the increased time as an opportunity to listen to and talk with the children individually and in small groups
- allocating more time for free exploration and play
- setting aside longer daily blocks of time for physical activity, for example, riding tricycles, running, jumping, skipping, climbing on apparatus (outdoors whenever weather permits)
- increasing the possibilities for first-hand hands-on experiences such as cooking and longer field trips
- including more frequent excursions in the neighbourhood and beyond
- reading to the children **several** times each day
- observing each child more frequently to discover interests, strengths, needs, and growth which in turn leads to further programming for that child
- noting the varying energy levels of the children and providing opportunities for breaks when needed
- providing a nutritious morning and afternoon snack
- informing parents/guardians about appropriate expectations for a full-day kindergarten child prior to implementation of the full-day kindergarten program
- providing a half-day program for children who find it difficult to adjust to a full-day program or whose parents/ guardians prefer a half-day program for their child
- providing additional funds for experiences such as trips, cooking, etc., and for the provision of the increased quantity of standard consumable items that will be required
- including the opportunity for a rest period for those children who may require such a time

*I think the full-day kindergarten holds tremendous promise for both children and teachers **IF** we hold fast to our knowledge about how young children learn; the time they need to explore, investigate, and discover; and the importance of a stimulating, inviting and responsive kindergarten environment.*

14. As you think back on the kindergarten year, what were some of the strengths and limitations of the program as you remember them?
Most of all, what I remember as the greatest strength was the emphasis that Sandra, Joan, and I placed on the development of strong interpersonal relationships. The three of us enjoyed and valued one another both personally and professionally, and we made certain that the children saw that. We also worked hard to ensure that the children enjoyed and valued one another, and we provided lots of opportunity for them to work and play together. We believed that it was important for us to establish a rapport with each child and to build trusting relationships. With some of the children this rapport and trust came easily; with others it took more time. And so we listened to the children so that we could get to know each well, and we involved ourselves in each child's learning so we could observe the child's ways, and guide when guidance seemed needed and appropriate.

Another strength was that we worked very hard to accept where every child was along the learning continuum—socially, physically, personally, intellectually, and spiritually. We tried our best not to compare one child with another or to value the talents or abilities of one child more than those of another. I have to admit that avoiding comparisons was not always easy, but I do believe that, over time, we did become more successful, and that the children felt good not only about themselves but also about their value to the group.

As well, I felt good about the following elements of the kindergarten year:
- that we encouraged the development of strong personal relationships with and among the children
- that we made a conscious effort to respect the children as sensitive and capable human beings (I remember the day when one of the children showed up at school wearing a T-shirt that read "Children are people too!" There is no question that the words served as a gentle reminder.)
- that we attempted to provide a broad-based, experiential learning environment and program specifically designed for the particular group of children we were teaching
- that we respected the children's right to make decisions and to think for themselves
- that the lack of pressure placed on children to be at a predetermined place by a certain time allowed them to grow and learn at rates commensurate with their personal development

- that three adults who, although very different in life background and teaching experience, were able to agree with such ease about philosophy, perspectives on child growth and development, and attendant programming for the young
- that we believed in activity and movement for young children—all children—and that we were able to design a program that supported this belief
- that our volunteer program added so much to the quality of the program and allowed for so many more learning opportunities for the children than would otherwise have been possible
- that the communication among the three of us was so productive, considering that time constraints prohibited us from doing as much as we would have wished
- that there was an unwritten, but quite obvious agreement that Sandra, Joan, and I wanted to work well together

And, of course, there were the weaknesses—the "limitations" or "areas of concern" as I prefer to think of them:

- *over stimulation—too much, too soon, too often:*

Because I am who I am, I have a tendency to want to do a lot in a short space of time. I have always been that way, and I probably will go on being so. As a teacher I find it hard to slow down my pace and to move more gently through the day with the children. Sometimes it may have been difficult for some of the children to keep up the fast pace.

- *at times I probably needed to be better organized:*

When working with a group of children I know that it's important to be well organized to help the program to flow in a logical fashion. By nature, I don't think that I'm a particularly well-organized person, and I have to consciously make a real effort to be so. I do know that I was always well prepared for the children—the planning chart was always ready, the materials and equipment were always in order, the room was always arranged with "a place for everything and everything in its place," the letters for the volunteers were always written, I was always on time and at the door when the children arrived each day. My organizational problems didn't begin until the children came through the door! Therefore, because my favourite phrase is "all of a sudden" and I enjoy the spontaneous and the unexpected, my favourite days were the ones that didn't go as The Planning Board (see pages 114-17) indicated they would. I hope the children enjoyed those days too!

What I did come to realize and accept was that, for me, it was important to be well organized in preparation for the children's arrival, and that careful and thoughtful planning was vital to ensure that no matter how the day unfolded there was always a written and visible reminder to help me get back on track.

- *the question of how much to introduce at a time—there were times when I think I asked too much of the children, expected too much of them, and I'd forget to ask myself, "How much can a young mind think about at any one time?" :*

It was sometimes difficult for me to know when enough is enough. As I have said, I have a tendency to do things quickly and I needed to remind myself to slow down a bit when I was with the children. The whole question of when does stimulation become over stimulation that may frustrate the children and when is it under stimulation that may bore them is something I had to keep thinking about. I know that I err on the side of over stimulation because I need to have a lot going on in my life all the time; however, I also know that some children function best in a more calm and peaceful environment. Bringing that balance to the program was something I thought about a lot—particularly as I planned each day and tried to ensure that delicate mix.

- *once we combined the three kindergartens, I found organizing the yellow room to be difficult:*

If I were doing it again, I'd work with Joan and Sandra to get the three groups of children and the three rooms working together by the end of September rather than waiting until December. To familiarize the children with the activities in the yellow room and the double room, and to help them to feel more comfortable about working anywhere in the kindergarten space, Joan, Sandra and I could rotate where each of us would begin our day with the children. For example, on Monday, Joan could start with her group in the yellow room while Sandra and I began with our groups together in the double room; on Tuesday, Sandra and her group could begin in the yellow room while Joan and I were in the double room; on Wednesday, my group and I could start in the yellow room while Joan and Sandra began in the double room. This arrangement would not only help the children to become familiar with and comfortable about working in the various areas in the kindergarten, but also the teachers! If the budget permitted, I'd have some of the wall between the yellow room and the big room knocked down and replace the door with a big arch. I'd make the yellow room a games room with large muscle activities and sufficient and diverse learning opportunities to attract all the children. For planning purposes, once we got the three rooms and the three groups of children working together, I would post a large, three-teacher-designed, cooperative chart to help keep everything coordinated:

- what centres?
- where?
- what will the purposes be for each centre and how will each centre work?
- who will be "in charge" of each centre?

I'd make a large map of the three rooms and pin cards on the map to tell what the learning centres would be for each week and where they'd be located. The cooperative chart and map would also be useful for the volunteers who so often came in each week and asked *"Where is the cut-and-paste centre this week?"*

- *and without question, I'd always remember to cover the paste and paints, and to clean the brushes!*

Part V:
Annotated Resources

During my year in the kindergarten and throughout my career in education I have found it extremely important to read professionally to keep up with what researchers and practitioners are telling me about current theories and thinking in education. Most jurisdictions have curriculum guides and they are filled with wonderful ideas for teaching the beginning years. But I think it's important that we read beyond the guides and beyond our jurisdictions. And although it's difficult to find a lot of outside readings that relate specifically to kindergarten, there are many fine books available that deal with the **spirit** of teaching and learning. These books give us, as kindergarten teachers, a direction for our thinking that will better ensure a consistency of philosophy between the program in kindergarten and the program in the early grades.

Following are a few books that I believe have something particularly valuable to say to kindergarten teachers. I hope you will enjoy reading them as much as I have.

Ashton-Warner, Sylvia. *Teacher*. Englewood Cliffs, NJ: Touchstone (Simon & Schuster International Group), 1986.

This captivating story is the author's account of her work with Maori children in New Zealand and of their early adventures in reading. This is an important book for all who are interested in how children interact with print in their early years.

Barron, Marlene. *I Learn To Read and Write the Way I Learn To Talk.* Katonah, NY: Richard C. Owen Publishers, Inc. No publication date is given; however, I obtained the booklet in 1991 and I think it was new at that time.

Each of the twenty-seven pages of text focuses on a different aspect of Whole Language. Examples of the content are as follows: "Why children like whole language so much," "How do young children become beginning readers and writers?" and "There's nothing pretend about 'pretend' reading." Child-made illustrations to support the text are included and each topic is discussed in three, four, or five short paragraphs! Not only is this a fast read for teachers, but the information can be used effectively for parent information workshops to help family members better understand what our programs are about and why we do what we do.

Bredekamp, Sue, Ed. *Developmentally Appropriate Practice in Early Childhood Programs Serving Children From Birth Through Age 8.* Expanded Edition. Washington, DC: National Association for Educators of Young Children, 1987.

The focus is on programming practices that grow out of a knowledge of the characteristics of young children and how they grow and learn.

Cambourne, Brian. *The Whole Story*. Richmond Hill, ON: Scholastic Tab Publications Ltd., 1988.

This is an important book for kindergarten teachers because it helps us to appreciate how theory and practice must be interwoven if we are to understand the complexities of language learning and the implications for programming. I value the inclusion of the case studies to illustrate both the theory and the practice; as well I appreciate the definitions for terms that are used, which help reduce ambiguity.

Cartwright, Carol A., and G. Philip Cartwright. *Developing Observation Skills*. Toronto, ON: McGraw-Hill Publishing Company, 1984.

This book covers a range of purposes for observation and includes chapters on methods of observing and record keeping. Examples of tallies, checklists, participation charts, and rating scales are included. The chapter on anecodotal record keeping includes ideas for preparing for anecdotal records, interpreting anecdotal records, and various anecdotal formats that can be used. The blend of theory, philosophy, and practical ideas make this book desirable for all teachers to have in their library of professional references.

Clay, Marie M. *What Did I Write? Beginning Writing Behaviour*. Auckland, NZ: Heinemann Publishers (NZ) Ltd., 1975.

Using examples and explanations, this still-in-print book details the writing behaviours of young children. The book helps teachers to focus on what young writers can do and to explain the process of writing from scribble to paragraph.

Dudley-Marling, Curt. *When School Is a Struggle*. Toronto, ON: Scholastic Book Services, 1990.

The title introduces us to the focus and content of the book. For many children school *is* a struggle—one that often begins in the early years. Dudley-Marling shares his insights, his observations, and his recommendations for helping children experience success in the beginning years.

Fisher, Bobbi. *Joyful Learning: A Whole Language Kindergarten*. Portsmouth, NH: Heinemann Educational Books, Inc., 1991.

The title says it all! This truly is an account of joyful learning for both the children and the teacher. The setting is kindergarten and the focus is on language development. The practices described are based on contemporary theory, and one gets a real sense of a kindergarten that is busy with the sounds of children engaged in productive and joyful language learning.

Forester, Anne D., and Margaret Reinhard. *The Learners' Way*. Winnipeg, MB: Peguis Publishers Limited, 1990.

I like this book because it talks to us about real practice based on current theory and research.

Froese, Victor, Ed. *Whole-language: Practice and Theory.* Toronto, ON: Prentice-Hall Canada, Inc., 1990.

By taking one aspect of language development or programming—for example, reading, writing, talking, drama, assessment—each of the authors has been able to focus on a specific area and to explore it on both a theoretical and a practical level. This is a practice-into-theory book.

Fulghum, Robert. *All I Really Need To Know I Learned in Kindergarten.* New York, NY: Villiard Books, a division of Randon House, Inc., 1986, 1988.

Most kindergarten teachers will have read this book—an account of some of the author's life experiences, each in its own way a reflection of Fulghum's learning in the kindergarten (see page 128 for a list of some of Fulghum's kindergarten learnings).

Napier-Anderson, Lois. *Change: One Step at a Time.* Revised Edition. Toronto, ON: University Guidance Press (OISE), 1991.

This book has won such a delightful response from teachers since it was first published in the late 1970s that, just recently, it has been revised to be more reflective of the contemporary educational scene. The author's intent is to describe the ten steps that she believes a teacher works through in programming towards a more integrated day. Although the book's applicability extends through the primary-grade years, kindergarten teachers will find the book useful not only in helping them to determine where they are along the continuum, but also in preparing for and implementing the next step in the process of change. For any teacher interested in learning-centre-based programming, this is must reading.

Newman, Judith. *The Craft of Children's Writing.* Toronto, ON: Scholastic Book Services, 1984.

Like others in the *Bright Ideas* Series, this book focuses on a single topic. In this case, the topic is the young writer. Samples of children's writing are provided and an explanation of what the child is telling us about his/her accomplishments is offered. Judith Newman's suggestion that we look at a child's writing by considering "intention, organization, experimentation," and "orchestration" is especially helpful to those who are looking for a consistent and humane way to assess and evaluate the young child's progress in writing.

Norris, Doreen, and Joyce Boucher. *Observing Children.* Toronto, ON: The Board of Education for the City of Toronto, 1980.

This book provides a comprehensive look at the intellectual/ language, social/emotional, and physical characteristics of children from ages two to thirteen. *Observing Children* is an important book.

Routman, Regie. *Transitions: From Literature to Literacy*. Portsmouth, NH: Heinemann Educational Books, Inc., 1988.

This book holds real appeal for me because it not only identifies the teacher's successes (and we all like to hear success stories!), but also we get to hear about the trials and tribulations that characterized this teacher "in change." And it's important and comfortable for us to know that change is not easy!

Schwartz, Susan, and Mindy Pollishuke. *Creating the Child-centred Classroom*. Toronto, ON: Irwin Publishing, 1990.

This book provides a comprehensive look at what is meant by "child-centred learning"—a term that to this point has often been very misunderstood!

Stauffer, Russell G. *The Language-experience Approach to the Teaching of Reading*. Second Edition. New York, NY: Harper & Row, Publishers Inc., 1980.

The use of children's life experiences as a basis for creating and developing reading opportunities highlights this text. The method is based on the premise that what one can think about and talk about can be written and read. If you are going to implement the approach described by Stauffer, you will need lots of experience chart paper and magic markers!

Van Manen, Max. *The Tone of Teaching*. Toronto, ON: Scholastic Book Services, 1986.

This *Bright Ideas* book examines a topic of importance to all teachers—the tone of teaching and the atmosphere for learning. The chapter titles reveal the tone of the book, from "Children Teach Possibility," through "The Experience of Curiosity and Wonder" to "Competence Is a Way of Being With Children." The author's sensitivity to children and for childhood is revealed on every page and the importance of the quality of the relationship that exists between adult and child is imbedded in every chapter. This book is useful reading not only for teachers but also for parents.

The books following also address topics and issues that affect kindergarten teachers and programming. Kindergarten and primary division teachers in my jurisdiction recommend them highly.

Baskwill, Jane, and Paulette Whitman. *Evaluation: Whole Language, Whole Child*. Richmond Hill, ON: Scholastic Tab Publications Ltd., 1988.

We all need as much information on this topic as we can get, so reading this book is a must!

Cohen, Dorothy, and Virginia Stern. *Observing and Recording the Behavior of Young Children*. Teachers College, Columbia University, New York, NY: Teachers College Press, 1983.

How to carry out the observing and recording processes is something we are always concerned about. This book is a great help.

Faber, Adele, and Elaine Mazlish. *How to talk so kids will listen and listen so kids will talk*. New York, NY: Avon Books, 1980.

Certainly the title suggests that all kindergarten teachers need and will want to read this book!

And my favourite professional reading of all—a little book of 47 pages:

Martin, Bill, Jr. *The Human Connection*. Washington, DC: Department of Elementary-Kindergarten-Nursery Education, National Education Association of Washington, DC, 1967.

This book has been out of print for several years now, but I wanted to include it because if you ever come across a copy you must make the time to read it. As the title suggests, the focus is on relationships and, in particular, on how a counter-productive relationship between a kindergarten boy and his teacher evolves into a positive human connection.